Praise for

GOD, GENESIS & GOOD NEWS

"Bull and Guy deftly untie the Gordian knot of science-faith conflicts by insightful reinterpretation of the Genesis text. This is a must-read for anyone concerned about beginnings in relation to the biblical record."

– *James Hayward*

"If you read the Genesis stories as if they were taken from the newspaper, you end up with information. If you read them the way Bull and Guy do, you end up with insight. And hope."

– *Charles Scriven*

Also by Brian Bull and Fritz Guy:

God, Sky and Land: Genesis 1 as the Ancient Hebrews Heard It

God, Land, and the Great Flood: Hearing the Story with 21st-Century Christian Ears

Understanding Genesis: Contemporary Adventist Perspectives (with Ervin Taylor)

GOD, GENESIS, & GOOD NEWS

BRIAN BULL & FRITZ GUY

ADVENTIST FORUM
adventistforum.org
Roseville, California

Adventist Forum
P. O. Box 619047
Roseville, CA 95661-9047
www.spectrummagazine.org

God, Genesis, & Good News

Cover and interior illustrations: Heather Langley
Design: Sharon Fujimoto-Johnson

Library of Congress Control Number:
ISBN: 978-0-578-60685-9

To our conversation partners who, through the years have complimented, criticized, and cajoled, and thus improved our literary efforts as well as our thinking. We are grateful for their unfailing friendship and support.

Table of Contents

Table of Contents

FOREWORD

THE "OTHER" WORLD OF GENESIS 1–11

This book is the final volume of a "retro-translation trilogy" addressing the ancient narratives documented in Genesis 1–11. We believe it is crucial that to be properly understood, all of Genesis, and especially the first eleven chapters, must be "retro-translated"—that is, expressed in words that reflect as accurately as possible the meaning conveyed to the original hearers. This is because the messages it contains were first addressed to ancient Hebrews living physically in the Land of Promise but existing mentally in (from our point of view) a parallel conceptual universe—an "other" world. Genesis was not initially addressed to us who now read it with great profit in the twenty-first century. Thus, in order for us to benefit now from the ancient Hebrew text, we must take into account the profound differences between our conceptual world and its concerns and the conceptual world and concerns of those to whom it was first addressed.

We are deeply indebted to those who lived in that very different world. We have access to Genesis only because they, in their search for the meaning of their existence, found immense value in a collection of ideas and insights enshrined in accounts of "the long distant past." Motivated by the Holy Spirit, they preserved, first orally and then in writing, those materials for their descendants. The literary form was usually a narrative—a story of God's interaction with their ancestors. Because these Hebrews invested a significant amount of their life energy and resources in memorizing, repeating, writing down, and copying these narratives, they are now accessible to us—translated, of course, for most of us. However, these narratives come to us from what was, in effect, a parallel conceptual universe. Because of this and because most of us read them in translation, some ramifications profoundly affect our understanding of both the narratives and their role in our modern Christian thinking. Even more important, these ramifications affect the role they should *not* play in our thinking but, unfortunately, often do.

As the third in this trilogy on the early chapters of Genesis, this book addresses challenges that face twenty-first-century Christians as we read and try to understand the narratives. All of us interpret the Bible every time we read it—notwithstanding claims to the contrary (such as "I don't *interpret* the Bible; I take it just as it reads"). The first two books attempted to reconstruct what the original audience of ancient Hebrews understood when they listened to, or read, the narratives of God's creation of material reality—the first Creation narrative (Gen. 1:1–2:4a) in *God, Sky & Land*,[1] and the Flood narrative (Gen.

1. Brian S. Bull and Fritz Guy, *God, Sky & Land: Genesis 1 as the Ancient Hebrews Heard It* (Roseville, CA: Adventist Forum, 2011).

5:29–9:17) in *God, Land, and the Great Flood.*[2] Those who first heard or read Genesis were the audience to whom Genesis was addressed, and what they understood is determinative for our twenty-first-century understanding. Their understanding will, at a minimum, set parameters for what the text can and should mean to us thousands of years later. If we are going to respect and internalize the message contained in these texts, we have no better place to begin understanding that message than to first find out what it meant to those to whom it was originally addressed. And of course, we will not stop there. We will apply what we learn there to our own thinking as modern Christians—but it is there and with them that we must begin.

The first two books of the trilogy asked, What could these parts of Genesis *not possibly have meant* to their original audience? This third volume addresses the subsequent questions, such as, Why at many points in the stories of Creation and the Flood is it so easy for twenty-first-century readers to ignore the ancient Hebrew world, that parallel conceptual universe, and remain in our own? Why is it that at various points in the ancient text, we seem to come across specific information about the world that seems self-evident to us who read it in the twenty-first century but would have made no sense at all to the original audience? How does it happen that the Biblical text seems to reflect our modern view of reality when it was written at a time when reality was understood very differently?

This far removed in culture and worldview from that ancient time period, it is difficult for us to figure out precisely what

2. Brian S. Bull and Fritz Guy, *God, Land, and the Great Flood: Hearing the Story with 21st-Century Christian Ears* (Roseville, CA: Adventist Forum, 2017).

the original audiences pictured as they listened to narratives of Creation and the Great Flood. Determining what the text *could not possibly have meant* to those who first heard or read it is much easier. For instance, they could not have visualized a heliocentric arrangement with a sun at the center of a solar system and planet Earth orbiting that central sun. Mental pictures of that sort have been possible only since the Copernican revolution about four hundred years ago. They would have been inconceivable to any ancient Hebrew minds. For the Hebrews it was obvious that the sun was much smaller than the land (*'erets*) where they lived and that it circled their land each day—a land that had been fixed in place by none other than God.

Another, more fundamental task has been waiting in the wings, namely, the challenge we acknowledged in the foreword to *God, Sky & Land*. It began, "We wish it were otherwise, but there is no getting around the fact that there is a profound disconnect between science (as commonly understood) and Genesis (as usually read), a disconnect that has existed since the scientific revolution began in the sixteenth century." In due course this final book of the trilogy will take up the challenge of that science-religion disconnect, but it first explores Biblical interpretation more generally. Finding out whether or not Genesis is being read and understood appropriately is a task that must come before finding out why it does not appear to support commonly accepted conclusions of modern science.

The approach we took in the first two books is essential to this task. There we *retro*-translated the Genesis narratives of Creation and the Great Flood from Hebrew into modern English. What was "retro" about our translation? It was our diligent effort to avoid using any English words or phrases that would evoke in the minds of modern readers the images, concepts, and/or ideas that would have been inconceivable to those for whom the Genesis narratives were originally composed—inconceivable because they did not yet exist.

ADDRESSING WHO AND WHY, NOT WHAT AND WHEN

When applied to the Genesis narratives of Creation and the Flood, retro-translation produces some remarkable results. The retro-translated narrative diverges significantly from the more familiar story even before the first verse of the Bible has concluded. To illustrate the divergence, we call again on two emblematic, imaginary friends—an ancient Hebrew, Moshe He'eb, and a modern twenty-first-century reader, Ian Michael O'Dern—both of whom first appeared in *God, Land, and the Great Flood* and will show up again in chapter 1 of this book.

In our scenario they are each anticipating answers to fundamental—but fundamentally different—questions. Moshe's questions were essentially theological: *Why* does the world—everything we see around us or know about—exist? *Who* is responsible for it being here? Does human life *mean* anything? Ian Michael's questions, by contrast, are historical and scientific: *When* and *how* did planet Earth come into existence? And *how long* has there been plant, animal, and human life on Earth?

Inevitably, the very different questions have very different answers. To Moshe's theological question Who? the answer, more than three thousand years ago, was simple and direct: *God.* God chose to create human reality in the divine image and thus to actualize God's will on the land.

Ian Michael, of course, is in an entirely different place. He has read that Creation began with water and darkness everywhere (Gen. 1:2), but he knows that could not have been literally the case because he has seen his home planet, a cloud-swathed blue sphere hanging in empty space—certainly not in water and darkness. Since Genesis (as he understands it) promises to inform him when heaven and earth came into existence, he expects at least some background information about the origin of his planet Earth, the star (which we know as the sun) around which it travels, the greater solar system, and perhaps the galaxy called the Milky Way. These two sets of questions and their expected answers could hardly be more different, and no single narrative could simultaneously satisfy both. Any conceivable account of beginnings will fail to address the expectations of either Moshe or Ian Michael. In light of what each hopes to get from the Creation narrative, the conceptual paths on which they travel diverge so far that an unbridgeable chasm lies between them.

This, then, is the challenge in reading and interpreting Genesis. To illustrate, we look at the sentence with which the English Bible begins. Genesis 1:1 is commonly translated, "In the beginning God created the heavens and the earth." When *retro-translated*, this familiar language becomes, "To begin with, God created the sky and the land." This is the beginning of a very different narrative, and in this book we explore where this different narrative takes Ian Michael as a twenty-first-century reader of the Bible's first chapter. Further, we attempt to explain how Ian Michael's creation narrative—which we believe to be profoundly mistaken—came to see the light of day; and, more important, why it is now necessary to scrutinize so carefully the Genesis account he reads and why it is necessary to carefully go through it word by word to remove the material that would have been unintelligible to the original audience—Moshe and his kin. In addition to exploring how this situation came about, we will look at why the disconnect between Genesis and science is so profound, and most of all, why the disconnect exists at all.

GENESIS IS THEOLOGY, NOT PRE-SCIENCE OR

PROTO-SCIENCE

A useful approach is to recognize Genesis 1–11 as fundamentally *theology*—words (in thinking and therefore in language) about divine intention and action. This was certainly the way the narratives were understood in Moshe's world, where the operation of nature had not yet been distinguished as a separate reality from God's direct action. For this reason it is imperative for us to keep in mind that Genesis, as originally written and initially understood, was wholly about *divine action*. Thus it was what we would call *theology*—certainly not *science* or *proto-science* or *history*. True enough, *theology* was not then an explicit category; it is our best term for Moshe's broader category—a much larger "tent"—than Ian Michael understands it to be, living as he does in the modern, scientific, and predominantly secular world. For Moshe, three thousand years ago, every thing and every occurrence that could not be explained as the result of human action was understood to be the result of divine action. If it rained, the explanation was that "God brought the rain." If a woman became pregnant, the explanation was that "God opened her womb." Thus the perception that "God had acted" served as an all-encompassing meta-explanation, including thinking and language about what we take for granted as *natural occurrences*, all of which were understood as *God's actions*. Today, of course, thinking and language about natural occurrences and the "laws of nature" fall into the very different category we know as *science*.

An example of this kind of theological meta-explanation occurs in Proverbs 16:33: "The lot is cast into the lap, but the decision is the Lord's alone." The careful reader notices that this is a statement of a general principle: the Lord (Yhwh) determines the outcomes of a process that twenty-first-century readers understand very differently—as belonging in the totally *nontheological* realm of probability theory. These readers find it strange indeed that Hebrew *theology* then included YHWH determining how thrown dice landed. This, however, precisely illustrates the parallel conceptual universe we need to enter in order to understand ancient Hebrew Scriptures as they would have been understood when they were first heard.

GENESIS IS ALSO HISTORY IN THE SERVICE OF THEOLOGY

We English speakers use and understand the word *history* in different ways, giving the word different, though clearly related, meanings. Sometimes, for example, we use the word to designate what has happened—some or all of the *events* of the past: we talk about "the history of the United States" and "the history of Christianity," or we recall that "Joe has a history of shady deals." At other times the word refers to a *record* (or *records*) of such events; we say, "Barbara is majoring in history" or "There's not much American history before the sixteenth century." At other, less frequent times the word refers to the subsequent *impact* of an event: "The invention of the hula hoop hasn't had much of a history."

But after an event has occurred, however significant or insignificant it may be, no one has direct access to it—not even the person or persons who participated in it or experienced it. All that remains is somebody's subjective record or one's own subjective memory—either of which is inevitably influenced to some extent by the limitations of human perception, perspective, and prejudice. So, strictly speaking, "objective history" is an unrealizable ideal. This is true even of Biblical history—and may bc *especially* true in the case of Biblical history because the writers were so personally and profoundly involved in their writing. They were anything but objective recorders of facts. They *cared*.

Moreover, the challenge of understanding Biblical history is yet more complicated because Scripture is a collection of *ancient* writings. Here again, we must take account of the historical—and specifically historiographical—context, which was significantly different from our modern context. Modern historiography and ancient historiography are profoundly different. That difference is captured effectively by a modern historian writing about ancient wars:

> Historical writing, which attempts to represent actual events by means of verbal narrative, and to construct a coherent story from a variety of more or less tractable raw data, is bound to be a distortion of reality. In this sense all history contains an element of fiction. . . . The way in which a historian bridges the gap between primary sources and finished (constructed) text depends on convention. The modern convention among professional historians is to make the relationship explicit, and as far as possible to indicate to the reader how the final product arises from the source material. It is further agreed that the historian must, if challenged, be able to support any and every statement with evidence. But in other genres (such as historical novels or biography), and in pre-modern historiography, there is much more leeway; writers are permitted to reconstruct, from their own imaginations, the feelings, aspirations and motives of persons and groups, to conjure up plausible scenes . . . and even to put their own words into the mouths of persons in the drama. These conventions were accepted without question in antiquity, when history was at least in part a rhetorical exercise.[3]

3. T. J. Cornell, *The Beginnings of Rome: Italy and Rome from the Bronze Age to the Punic Wars* (c. 1000–264 BC) (New York: Routledge, 1995), 17.

For the writers of Genesis, their work was both a rhetorical exercise and much, much more; it was a *theological vocation*. In the service of that vocation, they felt free "*to reconstruct, from their own imaginations, the feelings, aspirations and motives of persons and groups, to conjure up plausible scenes . . . and even to put their own words into the mouths of persons in the drama.*" To the extent that they were writing history, it was history in the service of theology.

GENESIS IN TRANSLATION

We face another problem in Biblical interpretation, a problem that would not occur at all if twenty-first-century Christians could read and understand Biblical Hebrew situated in its ancient context. Because most of us cannot do this and must rely on English translations, a translator and a translation necessarily lie between the Hebrew narrative and us.[4] This is not bad news; it is a blessing that we do not have to be fluent in Biblical Hebrew to hear God's Word in the Hebrew canon. It does, however, pose a challenge, because *every translation is an interpretation*. Translators of Scripture have no choice in the matter; interpretation is intrinsic to their task. To some extent the process of translation inevitably alters and sometimes obscures or even (in the worst-case scenario) distorts the meaning of the text.

Inherent in the translation and unavoidably interpretive process is the initial step in which a translator *hears* (understands,

4. A fantasy of one of the authors of this book is that in an ideal world, Christian students would learn Biblical Greek during middle school (grades 5–8) and Biblical Hebrew and Aramaic during high school (grades 9–12) so that by the time they enter college they would do their daily devotional reading of the Bible in its original languages. The result would be more direct access to—and much less misunderstanding of—the messages of Scripture.

comprehends, and thus interprets) what the Hebrew text is saying *to him or her*. This is where the problem begins, because two completely separate and distinct categories exist in a modern translator's mind. In one category are the Hebrew words about *divine action*; in a different category are the Hebrew words about *natural occurrences*. But these Hebrew words are read from a Hebrew text in which only one category existed. For the original author and audience, all of the words were about *divine action*; they were all *theology*. None of the words were about *natural occurrences* as the translator now understands this category. Because the narrative was intended for the first audience, it was neither science nor proto-science nor objective history; it was *all theology* and should be understood accordingly.

Obviously, this very "other" conceptual world from which the Hebrew text comes to us makes the translation process extremely challenging. Facing this challenge, translators, in a conscientious attempt to lessen the strangeness, often "update" the Hebrew text as they translate it—sometimes deliberately, sometimes unconsciously. Thus they make it less strange, but at the same time, they plant the seeds of the present conflict between Genesis and science. Our "retro-translation trilogy" attempts to reverse this process and thus re-create the other-worldliness portrayed in the Hebrew text. At the same time, we address the possibility that the long-assumed and much-argued Genesis-versus-science conflict may not actually exist. If so, then careful, thoughtful twenty-first-century readers of the Bible can turn their full attention to what the Bible tells us about God and thus avoid entirely the time-consuming, never-ending, friend-losing battles that have dogged readers of Genesis 1–11 for several centuries.

The changes required by retro-translation begin at Genesis 1:1, where the English word "land" (rather than the usual "earth") is employed to translate the Hebrew 'erets. The process of retro-translation requires this substitution of one English word for another because of what has happened in the past three hundred years that renders the word "earth" misleading in this context.[5] Here, and indeed in the majority of Biblical contexts where he encounters "earth," Ian Michael will almost always default to understanding "earth" as Earth, his home planet circling its parent star (which he knows as the sun) and held in its orbit by gravity. All these realities, evoked in his mind just by reading the English word "earth," were literally inconceivable and thus unavailable to the ancient Hebrews to whom the message of Genesis was addressed. It was they who, finding the text as they then understood it immensely valuable because it gave them relevant information about who God was, what God was doing, and what God wanted for them, began the labor-intensive process of copying and thus preserving the Creation narrative for posterity. We are part of that posterity. Although the text was not initially addressed to us, it remains God's Word to us and is, in that profound, if indirect, sense, *intended* for us.

Paired with *'erets*/earth in Genesis 1:1 is *shemayim*/ heaven. This Hebrew word is most often rendered in English as "heavens." Reading it, pluralized more often than not, evokes in Ian Michael's mind images of "starry heavens," "unnumbered galaxies," "the previously invisible realms of reality now brought clearly into view by the Hubble space telescope." For many modern Bible readers, the word *heavens* evokes the entire universe. But these cannot have been the

5. Thanks to the "ordinary language" movement in twentieth-century philosophy spearheaded by the Austrian-British philosopher Ludwig Wittgenstein (1889–1951), it is now widely recognized that the meaning of a word is determined primarily not by its linguistic origin (etymology) but by its common usage.

images conjured up in the minds of the original hearers and readers of the Genesis text because images of planets, unnumbered stars, galaxies, and galaxy clusters have become conceivable only comparatively recently. For this reason, to achieve a rigorously consistent approach to Biblical interpretation, a twenty-first-century believer must begin the process of reading and interpreting the Bible by keeping in mind the profound effect of word choices made by those who translated the Bible version at hand.

Reading a translated text, as most of us must, we need to keep constantly in mind that a translator's choices of appropriate English words are always conditioned by the images evoked in the translator's mind as he or she read the original Hebrew text. If, for example, on reading Genesis 1:1 the translator pictured the coming into being of our planet Earth, the solar system, and the universe beyond, then *shem-ayim* and *'erets* would become "heavens" and "earth." In that case, English readers of the translated text very likely picture planetary, solar, and galactic images too. Moreover, unless the readers of the English translation are extraordinarily introspective, they will imagine that their astronomical images are similar to the images that the ancient Hebrews mentally pictured—which, of course, is impossible.

The challenges of Biblical translation and interpretation are not new; they have existed for millennia. Arguments about interpreting the narratives began even before the Biblical canon was defined in first-century Palestine.[6] In early seventeenth-century Europe, however, with the power of science demonstrated—a formal analysis of empirical data and the codifying of nature's regularities—the challenges of Biblical interpretation

6. We know this from records of discussions about which extant scrolls were "canon-worthy."

began to press upon readers with increasing force. At that point in time, with the early stirrings of science within the community of scholars,[7] the sibling rivalry between science and theology began.

WHAT GENESIS IS

What then will be the outcome if we twenty-first-century Christians read Genesis as theology rather than as science or pre-science or proto-science? What would be the consequences if we read them as words about *divine action* (what God does) and ultimate meanings?

The fundamental question to be addressed can be stated simply enough: Is finite reality best understood as the gift of a loving God concerned about human flourishing? Or is it the chance outcome of random physical forces that, in the case of our particular universe, just happened to provide conditions favorable to life—including the remarkably coincidental characteristics of a "Goldilocks planet," not too hot or too cold, rotating not too fast or too slow, with gravity not too strong or too weak, and so on? Genesis is at the epicenter of this increasingly fractious debate. In this final volume of our retro-translation trilogy, we explore these questions by reentering the very different world from which Genesis comes to us.

7. The earliest "scientists" were known as natural philosophers.

CHAPTER ONE

THE VERY DIFFERENT WORLDS THAT WORDS CREATE

Simply Theology, Not Theology and Proto-science

The regularities of nature are prominent in our daily lives and in our understanding of reality in general. Thus it is that anyone reading the first Genesis Creation story in the twenty-first century may well assume that its language about "heavens and earth" (Gen. 1:1), "first day" (v. 5), "stars" (v. 16), "wild animals" (v. 24), "fish of the sea," and "birds of the air" (v. 26) constitutes a kind of sacred proto-science. Although this proto-science of millennia ago is by no means as rigorous and well defined as modern science, the Genesis account may seem to be referring to regularities in the natural world.[1] Though completely understandable,

1. These regularities are often called "laws of nature" because they were widely regarded as decreed by God and thus analogous to moral

this impression is a fundamental and far-reaching mistake. The message of Genesis 1 is not about natural realities and regularities; it is *about God and what God does*. God is the grammatical subject of most of the sentences and the implied subject of many of the others. In other words, Genesis 1 is properly understood not as proto-science but as words about divine action. It is, very literally, accurately, and significantly, theology and nothing else.

The widespread failure to recognize that Genesis 1–11 is theology—words about who God is, what God does, and what God wants for us, rather than some sort of proto-science or prehistory—is a result of the largely ignored difference between ancient Hebrew thinking and modern Western thinking. For us in the twenty-first century, words, discussions, and discoveries about the regularities of nature occupy a rigorously well-defined and completely separate category—the category we call "science." It may well be a very extensive and complicated category, but our minds have no difficulty distinguishing it from other categories, especially theology. For the ancient Hebrews, however, that was not the case. Since the category of science was still millennia in the future, for them, any talk about natural phenomena—whether a pregnancy, a flood, or an epidemic—belonged to the same category as talk about God and God's action in the world. All of this was *theology*.

Recognizing this difference between ancient Hebrew and modern Western conceptualizations is important because of a fundamental question that all Christians in the twenty-first century must address: how should we understand the Bible? In their devotional lives as well as their doctrinal beliefs, all Christians must decide how they are going to read and interpret

---

laws such as the Ten Commandments (Exod. 20:3–17).

Scripture. Interpretation necessarily precedes application; interpretation is intrinsic to understanding the Bible if what one learns by reading it is to make a difference in one's life. Proper interpretation requires not only understanding the individual words but also recognizing the nature of the material—not necessarily all of the specific details, but the intent and function of the content. Is it history, genealogy, instruction, prophecy, or something else? Unfortunately, this question is much more difficult to answer than it may appear because some parts of the Bible (such as Genesis) are several millennia old, and the categories into which these narrative writings may be classified today can be very different from those of the time when the writings were first committed to memory and/or clay tablets.

NARRATIVE ASSISTANTS: IMAGINARY BUT USEFUL

In our efforts to understand Genesis 1–11—and in the process needing to move back and forth between conceptualities that are separated by time, space, and culture—we need all the help we can get. Accordingly, in this chapter and in most of those that follow we will employ a couple of imaginary and symbolic figures. The readers of the second book in the trilogy, *God, Land, and the Great Flood*, have already met them, and they reappeared in the foreword to this book, where they proved helpful.

The first one is Moshe He'eb, who represents the ancient Hebrews but is himself middle-aged and in good health. He is bearded, and he carries a rough-hewn staff as he walks the rugged and dusty paths of various *lands* of the ancient world. We find him often enough in the Promised Land, but he is by no means limited to that locale. Moshe personifies the original hearers of the Biblical text and those who found its narratives, exhortations, prophecies, and other material useful in their quest to understand God and themselves more fully. Finding such material valuable, they recorded it for posterity. Moshe's contemporaries were the inspired authors and audience of Genesis.

Our second figure, less strange but equally imaginary and symbolic, is Moshe's modern counterpart, a college-educated and intellectually curious young man named Ian Michael O'Dern. He is clean shaven and casually dressed, a paradigmatic twenty-first-century Christian. He is a serious reader of the Bible; but since he doesn't know Hebrew, he has to rely on one or more modern translations. He represents almost all of us; and if his initials "I. M." are pronounced together rapidly with his surname "O'Dern," the result sounds (not coincidentally) like "I'm modern."

We hope that these two imaginary figures, representing times, cultures, and worldviews separated by almost three thousand years, will help to clarify their drastically different interpretations of the same Biblical text. They illustrate why a "retro-translated" Genesis, a version that employs only the information and conceptualizations that were available to Moshe, seems so otherworldly—why it was read and understood so differently *then* (by Moshe) from the way it is read and understood *now* (by Ian Michael—and by us).[2]

---

2. We recognize that both of these figures are male. Since (1) the English language is conventionally gendered and (2) contemporary anthropologists tell us that all known cultures are *patriarchal*, it seems the less misleading course for us to follow the custom of referring to humanity in general with masculine pronouns. For these reasons, our imaginary figures are both male. We regret that this may annoy some readers, but to make one male and the other female would imply differences more far-reaching than we intend (and more distracting!).

DIVINE ACTION, HUMAN ACTION, AND NATURAL REGULARITIES

Moshe's conceptual world included only two kinds of agents (or agencies), divine and human, which between them were responsible for everything that existed or happened. Divine agency was by far the more powerful and extensive. Moshe took it for granted that "what God did" accounted for most, if not all, of reality. In his view, what God did, along with what other supra-human agents (angels, for example) did, accounted for everything that mattered most. Everything else was attributed to the other class of agents: humans and, occasionally, other earthly creatures. Thus in the world from which Genesis comes to us, "what God did" and "what humans did" covered the waterfront. In the interest of verbal economy, and because we will be referring to them often in this book, we will continue our earlier practice and refer to these explanatory concepts, which together account for everything, as *explanacepts*.

Any explanacept—a broad, overarching category that helps to account for a significant portion of reality—coexists with the other explanacept(s) that helps to account for the remainder of reality. To be human is to require explanations—hence the incessant questions, Why? How come? What for? So explanacepts, functioning collectively, explain all of reality. Although Moshe had only two explanacepts, they sufficed, satisfactorily accounting for everything in his world.

Like Moshe's, Ian Michael's set of explanacepts is a complete, all-inclusive package. What one explanacept does not cover, another one does; collectively they cover everything. So if a new explanacept emerges—and a new explanacept has indeed emerged since Moshe's time—Ian Michael's understanding of reality is significantly different. Especially relevant to the difference between the way Moshe heard the

Biblical accounts of Creation and the Great Flood and the way Ian Michael hears them now is the new explanacept *nature*. This concept simply did not exist in the minds of ancient Hebrews (or any other humans of that time), so Moshe knew nothing of it. As an explanacept, it comprises all talk about natural forces and their regularities—in short, all words about natural occurrences—as distinguished from talk about divine or human action. "Natural" events and entities collectively form the subject matter of *science*.

We are in no way suggesting that Moshe was blind to happenings in the natural world. After all, he was probably a farmer and knew when to expect rain (the "former" rain in the fall and the "latter" rain in the spring), when to plant, and when to harvest. He also understood that a woman did not get pregnant unless a man "knew" her (was sexually intimate with her; Gen. 4:1).

So what was the problem? What limited his conceptual world to only two personally active agents? Why was the explanacept "nature" missing? Answer: the way Moshe thought was different from the way Ian Michael thinks. For Moshe, talk about natural events was part and parcel of talk about God; natural events were God's doing. Leah became pregnant because "God [crucially] opened her womb" (Gen. 29:31; 30:22, 23). That God was also responsible for Rachel's barrenness was accepted without question by both Rachel and by Jacob, her husband (Gen. 30:2). Sexual intercourse, however necessary for pregnancy to occur, was obviously not sufficient.

By contrast, for Ian Michael, natural phenomena are not at all the result of God's direct action. Indirectly, of course, God is the ultimate basis of all reality, and in this indirect sense is the ultimate "cause" of everything that happens; this distinction is recognized in traditional Christian theology as the difference between "primary" and "secondary" causality. But for Ian Michael, God and nature are separate, easily distinguished from each other and quite different categories of explanation. For Moshe there was no "nature-talk," only talk about God and talk about humans. An event that could not be explained by human agency (such as the Great Flood) was necessarily explained by divine agency; at that time, no other explanation was available.

TRANSLATORS AND TRANSLATIONS

But this is not the only problem that Ian Michael faces as he reads the Bible in the twenty-first century and endeavors to understand and apply what he reads. Since he usually cannot read the original Hebrew of the Genesis text, he has to rely on a translation. Moreover, since every translation is inevitably an interpretation, what he is reading is not the Genesis text itself but an interpretation that is simultaneously a very brief commentary. This is the case because there is seldom if ever an exact match between Hebrew words and the corresponding English words by which they are translated; the ranges of meaning of the corresponding Hebrew and English words almost never overlap perfectly. Even the same words in the same language can have very different meanings at different times. If, as is often the case, two or more English words might be serviceable equivalents for a particular Hebrew word, the choice of which to use depends on what seems "right and proper" to the mind and sensibilities of the translator. The translator chooses the English word(s) that best captures the Hebrew author's meaning as the translator understands (that is, interprets) it. In the process, the translator is inevitably influenced, perhaps unconsciously, by previous translations in the same or other languages.

These issues have been recognized ever since translation

from one language to another was first attempted on a large scale. Indeed, as nearly as we can now determine, the Hebrew Bible was the first major literary work to be entirely translated. The result, the Septuagint[3] in Koine Greek (subsequently the language of the New Testament), was produced in Alexandria, Egypt, in the third and second centuries BCE. That translation became authoritative, sometimes carrying more weight than the extant Hebrew text—presumably because the available manuscripts of the Septuagint were older and thus produced closer to the times when the original Hebrew texts were first written than were the surviving Hebrew manuscripts. (The original manuscripts, known technically as "autographs," had long since disappeared.) Another possible factor is that sometimes the Septuagint text simply made more sense to later translators.[4] Since copies of copies of copies of both the Hebrew text and the Septuagint have been made through the centuries and these extant copies can be compared today, there is thus substantial basis for regarding the Septuagint as a good, dependable (though inevitably imperfect) translation of the original text.

Thus Ian Michael is necessarily dependent on the mental pictures that the original Hebrew narratives produced in the mind(s) of the translator(s) of the version he now reads. Those pictures guided the choice of English words to represent the Hebrew words. When the Hebrew words were "theological"

---

3. Abbreviated as LXX, the name Septuagint (from the Latin *septuaginta*, "seventy") originated in the legend that seventy-two translators (six from each of the twelve tribes of Israel), working independently, produced identical versions of the whole Old Testament.

4. An example occurs in Gen. 4:15, where "therefore" in the Hebrew text was replaced by "not so!" in the Septuagint, which was followed by the Syriac and Latin (Vulgate) versions—and more recently in English by NRSV and NIV.

(as Ian Michael understands the term), the process is relatively straightforward and often not problematic. (He, being college educated and relatively sophisticated linguistically, recognizes that all human talk about God is necessarily analogical and therefore imprecise because God is utterly beyond human comprehension and representation in language.) But, when words that seem to Ian Michael to be about natural phenomena are intermixed with words about what are clearly divine actions, he has a formidable problem. In these circumstances, if he believes the choice of an English word is not a good choice, he can easily show it to be defective by fact-checking it against empirical scientific data. Since it is the case that *talk about God* and *talk about nature* are inextricably intertwined in the Genesis narratives, all translators face a daunting task. Still, if Ian Michael is going to read and understand Genesis 1–11, the text has to be translated from ancient Hebrew into modern words that he can read and understand. Even though he can read those modern English words, he has a challenge ahead of him that is far larger than he is probably expecting, for those words about divine action are inextricably interdigitated with words about natural phenomena. He is about to discover that Moshe's world is strange indeed.

Chapter Two

MOSHE'S WORLD IS SO "OTHER" IT IS ALMOST UNRECOGNIZABLE

Moshe's Scrolls Told Him That the raqia' *Confined the* tehom

As Ian Michael reads the (retro-translated) early chapters of Genesis, he realizes that Moshe's understandings of origins were, at least from his (Ian Michael's) perspective, very different and very strange—bordering on the bizarre. Moshe understood from his sacred scrolls that the sky above his head and the land beneath his feet were created by God for his benefit because God had freely chosen to create and took pleasure in doing so. So far, so good. Up to this point, Ian Michael has no problem with Moshe's conceptual understanding and mental pictures; he experiences no discomfort in relation to Moshe's world. Cognitive dissonance, however, awaits him.

In harmony with his sacred scrolls, Moshe believed that God had initially faced a very unpromising situation: before God created Moshe's sky (*shemayim*) and land (*'erets*), darkness and water already existed—everywhere. God had first attended to the problem of the darkness. It was "deep darkness" (Job 12:22), more ominous than the simple absence of light. The opening sentence of the first creation narrative promised that a world of sky and land was about to become real. But if that were ever going to happen, the all-encompassing darkness had to be overcome. As the Genesis account confirms, God did overcome the darkness: God spoke, and light came to be (Gen. 1:3).

Even more problematic than the darkness was the *water*—that was not just water as Ian Michael thinks of it but the terrifying *tehom* that had to be reckoned with. While not a serious challenge to God—the *tehom* was not a demonic counter-god, and God was obviously much more powerful—it was enough of a problem that "putting it in its place" was necessary if Creation were to proceed. Otherwise Moshe's sky and land could not become real. (The land, *'erets*, created on the third day, was *yabbashah*—dry ground.) Although not a serious rival to God, the *tehom* must have felt like a threat to Moshe, who understood that it was still there and at any time could return and destroy everything he knew. Thus the *tehom* was a kind of lurking "un-creator," always hanging, quite literally, over Moshe's head. In the days of Moshe's ancestors, it had broken out catastrophically to produce the Great Flood. That it would not do so again, overwhelming Moshe and his kin, was entirely dependent upon God being faithful to the promise in the heart of the Genesis story: "I will remember my covenant . . . ; and the waters shall never again become a flood to destroy all flesh" (Gen. 9:15).

Here Ian Michael parts company with Moshe. Try as he might, Ian Michael cannot imagine the state of affairs that Genesis assumes and articulates. He cannot conjure mental images to match what he reads in his modern English version. He knows there is no *tehom* above the sky, for he has repeatedly seen rockets pierce the blue dome above, traveling from the space centers where the rockets are fueled and launched. On their outward journey, the rockets encounter no mass of water (*tehom*). Ian Michael has followed the rockets' exhaust plumes on television, and he has seen the plumes diminish in size until they disappear. He also knows that there never was an actual sky-vault (*raqia'*) far above his head to protect him from the *tehom*. Utterly unable to visualize what Moshe so vividly understood and so clearly pictured, Ian Michael passes over the words attributed to God: "Let there be a dome in the midst of the waters, and let it separate the waters from the waters" (Gen. 1:6). To the extent that the *tehom* and the *raqia'* enter his consciousness at all, he ignores them as he moves on in the narrative.

As Moshe understood his ancient narrative, on Creation Day One God attended to the problem posed by the all-encompassing darkness. For Moshe's familiar world of sky and land to become real and visible, the oppressive darkness had to be overcome, and that had to happen early in Creation. So, as the Genesis account affirmed, God spoke, "and there was light" (Gen. 1:3). But there was still the problem of the *tehom*, and until that was solved, there was no going forward to bring into existence the promised sky and land. That, after all, was what the Creation account was about. That Moshe's land would soon appear had been confirmed by the very first words of the Creation narrative: "To begin with, God created the sky and the land" (OHV).[1] Accordingly, on Creation Day Two, God confined the tehom to its designated place above the raqiaʿ.

A RETRO-TRANSLATED NARRATIVE OF CREATION: NOT ABOUT "FORMING" FOLLOWED BY "FILLING"

Although we have merely scratched the surface of the Genesis narrative of Creation, the process of retro-translation has already substantially changed its central meaning from the usual interpretation. Because he is college educated and intellectually curious, Ian Michael has heard more than once that the Creation narrative is about "forming" during the first three days and "filling" during the second three days. In other words, he understands that God first produced the entities of the newly created reality, entities such as the land and the sea that were to be filled, and then during the next three days He created the animals and humans to fill the land and the fish to fill the sea. In Ian Michael's world, the sun, moon, and stars, along with the land and sea, are part of the natural realm; this whole process makes good sense. "Forming" must precede "filling" because "natural" entities that do not exist cannot be further elaborated.

So the idea of "forming and filling" is perfectly reasonable. Besides, it is obvious to any observant reader that Day One saw the creation of *light* and Day Four saw the creation of *lights*. Day Two saw the separation of primeval *waters* (by the *raqiaʿ*), and Day Five saw the creation of *water creatures*. Day Three saw the appearance of *dry land*, and Day Six saw the creation of *land creatures*.

1. Our attempt to "translate" modern readers back into an ancient conceptual world (hence "retro-translation") results in a version of the Scriptures we call the Original Hearers' Version (OHV).

Furthermore, the alliterative formula "forming and filling" is a handy mnemonic device, helping students in a high school or college Bible class remember what happened on which days in the Creation narrative.

Nevertheless, like many simple formulas and memory aids, "forming and filling" is an oversimplification that deserves to be taken with a grain of salt. Light is hardly a "formation" that was "filled" by the sun, moon, and stars. Whatever the *raqia‘* was, it was not "filled" with water but, rather, served to confine water. And the land began to be *filled* with vegetation on the same day it was formed. Only in the case of the land *filled later* by animals and humans does the formula "forming and filling" actually work as a description of the actual Creation account in Genesis 1.

Moshe's narrative was different from Ian Michael's. Moshe took seriously the statement of Genesis 1:2 that "in the beginning" water and darkness were every*where* and constituted every*thing*. This being the case, God began the process of Creation by first dealing with these two problematic realities. Indeed, there is a sense in which, as Moshe understood the story, the actual production of material reality did not begin until Creation Day Three. As told in the Creation narrative, God had, on days one and two, addressed and corrected the pre-Creation state of affairs by dissipating the antecedent darkness with the introduction of light on Day One and by confining the pre-Creation waters with a *raqia‘* ("vault" or "dome") on Day two. By Day Three the unsatisfactory pre-Creation situation was rectified, and Creation could proceed with the creation of sea, land, vegetation, living creatures, and humans.

Ian Michael's Creation narrative is so different because he takes it for granted that what he is reading about is the coming into being of *astronomical entities* like planets, suns, and interstellar space as well as *terrestrial entities* like animals, birds, and human beings. He knows that the earth and other planetary bodies exist in empty space. Thanks to the Apollo 8 mission in 1968, he has seen the Earth hanging in space, suspended by gravity, a cloud-swathed blue sphere, looking fragile and vulnerable. When he reads that "the earth was a formless void, and darkness covered the face of the deep, while a wind from God swept over the face of the waters" (Gen. 1:2), the obvious meaning of the text—that water and darkness were every*where* and every*thing*—makes no sense to him. He therefore dismisses it as antiquated proto-science not worth further consideration. He knows that there is not water everywhere in space and that there never was. He also knows that star*light* from innumerable blazing suns pervades and illuminates the entire universe. At the same time he fails to appreciate what should be obvious by the second sentence: that what he is reading is *theology* (what the transcendent God does), not *science* (how the natural order functions). Because of this failure of perception, the way he thinks about the rest of the Creation narrative is fundamentally flawed.

Ian Michael also does not notice that there is no trace of God creating *out of nothing* in the Genesis narrative or anywhere else in the entire Hebrew canon. This idea first appeared during the intertestamental period, became common in New Testament times, and, ever since, has been part of most Christian understandings of Creation.

THE DIFFERENCE BETWEEN MOSHE'S "GREATER LIGHT" AND IAN MICHAEL'S "SUN"

Let's go back to Moshe, for it was to Moshe that Genesis was addressed. He understood that after God made "dry ground" (*yabbashah*) possible by confining the tehom above the raqia' and confining the surface water to "seas," God filled the dry ground with growing plants. He further understood that God next created a "greater light," a "lesser light," and "the stars" (Gen. 1:16). For Moshe's environment to be productive—for plants to grow and for Moshe himself to survive on the land God created for him—there had to be sunlight. God had created the "greater light" for this very purpose. God placed (the Hebrew word meant "firmly emplaced" or "set") it in the *raqia'* that He had created to protect Moshe's land from the *tehom*. This "greater light" was the essential timekeeper of Moshe's world, created by God to inform him of the special times for religious celebrations as well as to mark off the passage of days and years (Gen. 1:14). In every sense that Moshe could understand, the "greater light" was placed there by a benevolent God for Moshe's benefit. It traveled over Moshe's land every day to enable him to tend his fields and flocks and herds. It was there to serve him and whatever was his. A gracious God had created a world defined by the sky above and land beneath, all benignly overseen by the "greater light" for Moshe's benefit.

For Ian Michael the situation is entirely different. He is fully aware that Moshe's "greater light" is the sun, but it is not in any sense confined to a specific place in in the *raqia'*. Compared to Earth, Ian Michael's sun is an enormous astronomical body that at some time in the cosmic past pulled planet Earth into orbit around it and has kept Earth there for billions of years. Ian Michael knows that if the scientists he consults from time to time are correct, the sun will hold the Earth in solar orbit for billions of years to come.

So Ian Michael's sun is by no means the same as Moshe's "greater light." That "greater light" was tasked by God not only to light up the land but also to function as a timekeeper so that Moshe could tell when the "designated times" came around and would thus be less likely to miss the religious festivals that structured his life. It was also to serve as a timekeeper as the twelve divisions (hours?) of each "daylight day" passed.[2] "But," Ian Michael objects, "a daylight day would not have been exactly twelve hours long. Everyone knows that a daylight day is longer than twelve hours in the summer and shorter in the winter. Besides, the farther north or south Moshe went for whatever reason, the greater the disparity would be. If he had chanced to go far enough north or south, he might even have ended up with a daylight day that was twenty-four hours long!"

And that is where the strangeness of Moshe's Creation story has Ian Michael completely baffled. Could the two of them meet (a practical impossibility, of course, since they are separated by three millennia), Moshe might explain to Ian Michael that, yes, he (and everyone else) knew that the days were longer in summer, but they were still twelve hours long because an hour was defined as exactly one-twelfth of the time it took the "greater light" to go across the sky from sunup in the east to sundown in the west. In other words, an hour was going to be just as long or as short as the "greater light" defined it to be. There was no problem because it was the "greater light" that determined the passage of time. Since sunrise, noon, and sunset were easily observed, time was structured accordingly. That was why God created the sun in the first place. Noon, the sixth hour, was when the "greater light" was directly overhead. The

2. It is not even certain that early in the Hebrew Bible "hours" marked off the daylight day, although this was clearly the case by the time of the New Testament (Jn. 11:9). The term hour first appears in Daniel (Dan. 3:6, 15; 4:19, 33; 5:5), but this is not Hebrew and very few modern translations agree with the KJV that "hour" is what the Aramaic word means.

first hour began at sunrise; that was how day was understood to have begun for a very long time before Moshe came along. The twelfth hour—and the day—ended when the "greater light" disappeared in the west.

In a world without other means of keeping time, the sun *defined* the passage of time; that was its God-appointed purpose. That continued to be its role for hundreds of years until clocks (mostly water clocks) were common enough that an hour did not have to be defined by the sun directly. Surprisingly, however, since the water clocks had to be calibrated by sun dials, they too, for centuries, still marked out hours that varied in length from one day to the next.[3] Although there is evidence that in some places in the Roman Empire hours of fixed length were employed, it was not until the invention of mechanical clocks in the thirteenth century CE that sixty-minute hours became commonplace. Still, it took a while for the idea to become generally accepted, as portable timekeepers (functioning like modern watches) were far more expensive than "telling time" by the sun. Thus in the New Testament, while some nighttime events are reported in terms of hours,[4] others are located much more approximately (and much more traditionally) according to which of the four night watches was underway when an event occurred.[5]

Accustomed as he is to an hour of fixed length and a day of twenty-four hours of the same length summer and winter, Ian

3. See Jo Ellen Barnett, *Time's Pendulum: The Quest to Capture Time—From Sundials to Atomic Clocks* (New York: Plenum, 1998), 39, 40: "People in the ancient world were not ready to abstract time from the central reality of the sun's daily passage. . . . The calibration marked on the water clocks set beside sundials are not the simple equidistant lines that would make sense to us; rather they are a translation into water clock format of the readings given by the sundial."

4. Acts 23:23, NRSV; compare NKJV.

5. Luke 12:38, NKJV; Matt. 14:25, NKJV; Mark 6:48, NKJV.

Michael finds all of this strange indeed. He needs to remind himself repeatedly that he is reading a message that was not initially addressed to him but was "forwarded" to him like a time-transcending email. He is reading it because Moshe and his contemporaries found the message valuable in enhancing their understanding of God. They found it sufficiently valuable that it was copied and recopied for centuries—millennia, in fact—and that is why it is even possible for Ian Michael to now be confused[6] as he reads.

Moshe's world lacking, as it does, any knowledge of "natural" happenings is strikingly "other." Failure to appreciate the extent of this "otherness" has led to yet another confusion of categories. Not infrequently the Ian Michaels of the present time assume that descriptions of entities or events in physical reality from Moshe's time are to be understood in the way that similar events or entities would be understood and described today. In turn, this has led to the idea that both descriptions can be assumed to be "reference works" as, today, we attempt to get an ever tighter grasp on "the way things really are." Take, for instance, the proposition that Moshe's "greater light" and Ian Michael's sun, since they are referring to the same entity, can both be relied upon to further a "scientific" understanding of the "sun entity" in the twenty-first century. But as already noted, Moshe's "greater light" and

---

6. In an apparent attempt to be helpful (and lessen the probability of a confused Ian Michael), the NRSV has not translated the actual Greek text but instead rendered its meaning in modern English. Thus, in Acts 23:23 the "third hour of the night" (NKJV) has become "nine o' clock tonight." This is an apt illustration of the dilemma that all translators face. By making the text more immediately meaningful to Ian Michael, they have inveigled him into believing that the world of the New Testament was more like his twenty-first-century world than it actually was. The translation has muted the signals in the biblical text that early in the first century BCE a profound shift was underway in measuring and recording the passage of nighttime.

Ian Michael's sun are incommensurate. Only Ian Michael's sun is a nuclear-fueled star around which an entire solar system revolves. This potential confusion between entities existing in Moshe's "other" world and entities by the same name existing in Ian Michael's world (understandable though it is) deserves further examination before Ian Michael gets too engrossed in exploring the Genesis narratives.

THE ALLEGED COMPLEMENTARITY OF GOD'S "TWO BOOKS"

Ian Michael has often heard the claim that God's "two books" describe reality—the book of nature and the book of revelation. Without further thought he has accepted this as a truism. It sounds plausible, and it credits God as the foundation of all that exists. But does this truism hold up under inspection? It may be a truism, but is it true?

The circumstances that typically surround this oft-repeated claim suggest that a closer inspection may be worthwhile, for it is a claim that is most often advanced in situations where nature and revelation seem to be at odds, and it is adduced as an affirmation of an underlying but presently unapparent unity. If the idea of two books by the same author is most often invoked when nature and revelation appear to disagree, it seems likely that reality may be larger and more complex than this metaphor adequately reflects.

There are two obvious problems with the metaphor of "God's two books" as a representation of reality. The first is that at the time of the writing of Genesis (which begins the book of "revelation"), only two kinds of active agents were understood to exist. Moshe recognized that humans could (and did) do many things. Although he did not have the terminology we have today, he did not doubt the reality of what, during the intervening centuries, has come to be called "free will." Humans (and sometimes animals) were responsible for much of what happened. Everything else was attributed to God, in whose image humans had been created. The surviving writings of the ancient Hebrews make it clear that, as far as they were concerned, it didn't just rain; when water fell from the sky it was a direct act of God, and they described it accordingly: "I [YHWH] will cause it to rain" (Gen. 7:4, NKJV).[7] When quail arrived in the Israelite camp it was, likewise, a direct act of God and clearly identified as such:

> They asked, and [God] brought quails,
> and gave them food from heaven in abundance.
> (Ps. 105:40).

On a subsequent occasion when another flock of quail arrived in the camp, it was similarly understood as a direct act of God: "Then a wind went out from [YHWH], and it brought quails from the sea" (Num. 11:31). This time, however, there was a problem: the quail meat proved to be lethally toxic. Since the arrival of the quail had been attributed to God, the resulting lethality had to be attributed to God, too, and no one at that time and place thought a straightforward factual statement about YHWH bringing in quail was in any way strange. Talk about God's actions and talk about natural occurrences were logically parallel.[8]

Ian Michael, however, lives in a conceptual world that finds these statements strange indeed because he thinks in

---

7. See also Exod. 9:18; Lev. 26:4; Deut. 11:14; 28:12; and many references in the books of 1 and 2 Samuel, 1 and 2 Kings, 1 and 2 Chronicles, Job, and Psalms.

8. For a more complete consideration of this particular episode, see Bull and Guy, *God, Land, and the Great Flood*, 50–54.

terms of a third category, "nature," which includes talk about natural regularities and which he now refers to as God's "second book." In his world, these three active agencies—divine, human, and natural—explain everything that happens and are therefore fundamental to the way he and all of us, his contemporaries, think. These concepts inform and control the way he understands reality and into which he can fit everything. For that reason we have called them (perhaps a little clumsily) explanacepts. While Moshe thought with only two explanacepts, Ian Michael thinks with three. So, when reading and interpreting Genesis, Ian Michael is reading and interpreting a two-explanacept narrative with a three-explanacept mentality.

The complications for Ian Michael, however, run far deeper, because Ian Michael's "book of nature" contains many events and entities that were included in Moshe's "book of revelation," in which God-talk and nature-talk were inextricably intertwined. Moshe's book of "revelation" (the Hebrew canon) is an essential part of Ian Michael's book of "revelation" (the Christian Bible). So Ian Michael must confront this intertwining of words about God with words about natural events even though they are, for him, two separate and distinct explanacepts.

IAN MICHAEL'S PROBLEM THAT MOSHE DIDN'T HAVE

Ian Michael's thinking includes a vast amount of information about natural regularities. As a result, he thinks of rain not as God's direct action but as part of a normal hydrological cycle. He is aware that the Mediterranean Sea is vast and that European migratory quail will likely be exhausted after flying south over that watery expanse each year. Thus he will understand the arrival of a flock of exhausted quail on the southern shore as a natural annual event. The quail fly south each autumn to overwinter in sub-Saharan Africa. Trying to harmonize realities and entities in the natural world that are present simultaneously in both of Ian Michael's "two books," but as "God talk" in one book and "nature talk" in the other, will, not surprisingly, prove challenging for him.

Fortunately, however, harmonization is not difficult if Ian Michael can read and understand Moshe's account for what it actually was and is. It may well contain words about phenomena that are, for Ian Michael, natural regularities, but for Moshe, they were part and parcel of "what God does," so that any mental or oral consideration of them was "God talk." Because these phenomena were understood as theology—as part of what God does—that is how they were reported.

That a "face value," or literal, reading of the opening chapters of Genesis lies at the base of the Genesis/science conflict is so widely recognized that it may seem pointless to explore it in any more detail. Still, an exploration of the reasons why Ian Michael's Genesis differs so markedly from Moshe's and coexists so uncomfortably with what Ian Michael understands about science would seem to be a worthwhile undertaking.

As Moshe heard or read the narrative of Genesis 1, he learned that his world of sky and land had come into existence by the will and action of God, the transcendent, ultimate Reality. He learned something about who God is, what God does, and what God wants for human beings. He learned that his own existence had meaning—possibly transcendent meaning—because it was the result of the action of an Ultimate Reality who wanted him to exist and flourish and who freely chose to bring him into being.

Moshe came to understand God's action and motivation by reading words about God intermingled with words about the natural world. This combination of God-talk and nature-talk did not surprise Moshe at all, much less puzzle him; it was the way he had always understood his world, based on the stories he knew from childhood. The regularities of nature were the actions of the same God who heard and responded to Moshe's ancestors: "They asked, and he brought quails" (Ps. 105:40). This intermingling of words about God with words about *natural regularities* was in no way surprising or jarring to Moshe. As he understood it, both actions were part of "what God does."

Ian Michael, on the other hand, suffers from severe cognitive dissonance (a "brain-cramp") upon reading these words if he tries to understand what they mean. Being college educated, he understands all of the words about quails as words about *nature's regularities*. He understands them as belonging in "God's book of nature." To see these ideas juxtaposed in the same sentence with words about God he finds jarring—so jarring, in fact, that he probably does not even try to process the ideas on the page before him. Not having a conceptual category into which this juxtaposition of unlike ideas can fit, he sees the words but more than likely does not think seriously about them. For him it is like reading a foreign language; indeed, semantically it is a "foreign language."

This situation is understandable but regrettable. Failing to explore what might be causing cognitive dissonance as he reads the report of God's direct intervention in providing food for the meat-craving band of escaping slaves, Ian Michael is ill prepared even to identify words about God intertwined with words about *natural regularities* when he reads them elsewhere in Genesis. Not seeing these words as *theology*, he has no alternative; he has to consider them as *science* (or pre-science or proto-science). This mistaken identification only worsens in Ian Michael's mind the disconnection between Genesis and science, widening it to an unbridgeable chasm. Not adequately understanding ancient Hebrew narratives, not seeing them through Moshe's eyes, he lacks the necessary mental constructs with which to proceed.

If Ian Michael is going to enter this strange world that Moshe inhabits and, to some limited extent, hear the Genesis narratives as Moshe first heard them, he is going to need some tools for the task. It is to those tools for reading that we turn next.

Chapter Three

THREE TOOLS FOR MEANINGFUL READING

A "Close Reading" of the Text

In this book we have proceeded on the assumption that Ian Michael will have fewer problems when reading and interpreting the Bible generally and Genesis 1–11 in particular if the English version he reads has resulted from a "close reading" of the original Hebrew text. We believe that at least some of the difficulties that beset usual translations are eliminated (or substantially lessened) by this process. It is a "reading" that looks very closely at what the Hebrew text very literally says and, on the basis of that careful inspection and analysis, determines as far as possible *what the original authors' words actually conveyed to the original audience*. It is the first step in the retro-translation process.

A "close reading" takes for granted that the Hebrew words in the text were intentionally selected and that other

Hebrew words were sometimes intentionally passed over—even though they might seem to twenty-first-century English readers to have been better choices. In other words, it is an attempt to counteract the understandable but misleading tendency to suppose that the ancient Hebrew authors meant by their words *then* what we mean *now* when we use our corresponding English words.

In *God, Sky & Land* we observed that the Hebrew author of Genesis 1:1–2:4a used a cardinal number ("one") to designate the initial day of creation but used ordinal numbers ("second," "third," and so on) for the succeeding days. Noting this, we speculated about possible reasons for what, for us, is an unexpected choice. It is, we propose, the job of the retro-translator to identify textual curiosities of this sort, to draw them to the reader's attention, and also, if possible, to suggest their possible significance—what the author might have had in mind.

Here we note that the Hebrew as well as the Septuagint text of Genesis 1:1 (regularly translated as "In the beginning God created") lacks the definite article (*the*) before the noun (*beginning*). Observing that the definite article is absent from the original but has been regularly added to English translations of this verse, with the help of Moshe and Ian Michael we explore why this might be the case. Was the omission by the Hebrew author and Greek translator(s) intentional? Was the insertion by successive English translators intentional, or were they simply following the example of previous translations going back to William Tyndale's translation in 1530, and even back to the Wycliffe Bible translation of the Vulgate into Middle English in the late fourteenth century?[1]

---

1. In chapter 4 we explore this question in much more detail and consider what might be implied by the insertion. Evidently the Hebrew author of Genesis 1:1 had no general aversion to the definite article; he used it twice just a few words later to introduce both *shemayim* ("the" sky)

In this particular instance, the absence of the Hebrew definite article *ha* ("the") between the preposition *be* and the noun *reshith* ("beginning") in the word bereshith makes our retro-translated English rendering different from previous English translations. The result ("To begin with") reflects the Hebrew text more precisely, thereby muting the solemnity and emphasis of the verbal fanfare "In *the* beginning."[2] Thus, as early as its second word, a retro-translation of Genesis 1:1—an attempt to recapture what Moshe originally heard—has recognized that Ian Michael's path diverges, if only slightly so far, from Moshe's.

A "close reading" of the Creation narrative does not assume that something exists unless and until it is mentioned and does assume that it exists after it is mentioned. For example, "darkness" (*hodesh*) and "the deep" (*tehom*, Gen. 1:2) are described as already existing when the process of Creation began. Both are therefore to be understood as pre-Creation realities; and although both were relativized during the ensuing Creation week—darkness by the creation of light and "the deep" by the creation of the "vault" or "dome" (*raqia'*)—neither was part of what was brought into existence during the Creation week. Thus, according to a "close reading" of the narrative, neither was part of the Creation process described in Genesis 1.[3]

This approach assumes that when Genesis 1 defines an entity, that is the proper definition of that part of created

---

and *'erets* ("the" land).

2. An even more exact translation would be "Beginningly God created," but this is not standard English usage. "Initially God created" would work, but we think "to begin with" helpfully maintains the Hebrew emphasis on the beginning of the process.

3. Contrary to the implication of the traditional Latin formula *creatio ex nihilo*, the Genesis account of Creation does not in fact begin with the existence of absolutely nothing.

reality. Here we encounter an interesting but rarely noted implication of the generally accepted principle of letting Scripture function as its own interpreter. Thus when Scripture says that something exists, that entity exists and continues for as long as Scripture indicates that it does; for Scripture, more often than not, is our only source of information in such matters. In chapter 5 we take up the translation of *yom* ("day"). The text carefully specifies, "God called the light Day, and the darkness he called Night" (Gen. 1:5). There is no getting around this Scriptural definition: the Genesis "day" is the *light portion* of a light-dark cycle, and the *dark portion* is the "night." So a Genesis "day" is as long as day*light* lasts; it is not twenty-four hours long.

The idea that a day in Genesis might not be twenty-four hours long seems strange indeed to Ian Michael, who takes it for granted that, strictly speaking, a day is, and always has been, twenty-four hours long. (The word *day* is, of course, sometimes used adjectivally to signify a shorter period, as in "a day's work" or "a day's drive"; but even then it refers to a shorter period that occurs within a twenty-four-hour period.) A "close reading" of the text requires that a day is as long as Scripture states that it is. Such unexpected outcomes are precisely the sort of thing that retro-translation uncovers, relying as it does on how the ancient Hebrew actually reads, unmodified by twenty-first-century knowledge.

RETRO-TRANSLATION

The goal of retro-translating Genesis is that nothing in the resulting English version will convey to Ian Michael ideas that Moshe could not have had or even imagined because they were not conceived of by any human until long after Moshe first heard the Genesis narrative. So our neologism "retro-translation" has yet another meaning: it is not simply a translation of an ancient text into the modern world but also an attempt to "translate" modern readers *back* (hence "retro") into an ancient conceptual world. These are two reasons why we have named the version of Genesis that results from this retro-translation process the Original Hearers' Version (OHV).

As already noted, retro-translation requires that the Hebrew Bible itself should be the primary place in which to search for an understanding of the Biblical text. This wise course of action is virtually forced upon translators because of the paucity of extra-Biblical ancient Hebrew. The largest single source of the language of the Old Testament is the Old Testament itself. Since there is so little ancient extra-Biblical Hebrew material extant, to determine what a Hebrew word or phrase meant in a particular sentence, the translator must look at what it meant in other places *in the Hebrew Bible*. If the translator can ascertain its meaning in this way, that is all to the good. Fortunately, only rarely is this impossible, so that a word or phrase must be interpreted by its usage in extra-Biblical sources. Possible twenty-first-century meanings of such words or phrases—whether present in modern Hebrew or derived from current English, French, German, and other contemporary languages—are eliminated from consideration if they involve concepts that first emerged centuries after Moshe's era.

An instance of this phenomenon occurs as early as Genesis 1:10, in which Moshe heard that *'erets* ("land") was the name given to "dry ground." This was (and is) not surprising because he had heard at the start of the Creation narrative that God created the sky and the land. That the land was composed of "dry ground" was to be expected, and that it was described as "dry" ground was understandable too. After all, God had started the Creation process with water everywhere, with no "dry ground" in sight.

Ian Michael, however, has great difficulty equating "earth" with "dry ground." Nine verses earlier, he is informed that God created the "earth." He has understood that word *earth* as planet Earth for all of his life and now doesn't know quite what to do. He cannot mentally equate his home planet (where, as he learned in elementary school, oceans cover about 70 percent of its surface) with "dry ground." This is the kind of problem that arises when translators ignore the Scriptural definition of a Hebrew word ("dry ground" = *'erets,* land) in favor of a twenty-first-century definition—when Scripture is not allowed to interpret itself, even though it provides a perfectly clear definition of a common Hebrew word.

EXPLANACEPTS

The third tool for a meaningful reading of Scripture is the concept of explanacepts. Moshe's mind was equipped with only two, but the minds of all Hebrew-to-English translators in the past four hundred years have invariably employed three. So the original two-explanacept narratives are read by three-explanacept minds. We have already encountered an example of this phenomenon in the surprising (to us) pervasiveness of *theology* we observe in a two-explanacept world.

Consequently, several important questions await the careful twenty-first-century English reader who opens a Bible and begins to read Genesis 1:

- Does what I am reading contain any ideas, concepts, propositions, or entities that were inconceivable to those to whom these narratives were originally addressed? In other words, would everything have made sense to Moshe? Would the narratives have made enough sense for him to commit them to memory and laboriously record them, thus preserving them for his descendants? Would the descendants, in turn, find them so valuable that they would treasure them and recopy them for posterity?

- Do the propositions and concepts contained in these sentences fit comfortably into the only explanatory categories available to people in the ancient world? In particular, are there any statements about the phenomena of the physical world collectively, including plants, animals, the landscapes, and other features and products of the earth, as opposed to humans or human creations—that is, statements that appear to be about "nature" that are not attributed directly or indirectly to divinity-in-action?
- Am I mentally prepared to read Biblical statements about the *natural world* as *theology*? Can I exert the necessary mental effort to read them as statements about what God was understood (by Moshe) to do?[4] (This is a particularly difficult awareness to maintain, and most modern readers have little or no experience in trying to do so.)

Since the Genesis narratives were *composed as theology*, if Ian Michael truly respects the text he is reading, he will *read*

4. If Genesis is to be understood now as it was originally, statements about the behavior and/or appearance of rain or quail or a devastating Flood have to be read as statements about what (in those times and places) God was understood to have done directly. At that time and place there was no intervening "realm of nature."

them as theology. Because, however, he has consistently read it as science (or proto-science) for all of his life, this challenge is especially formidable; but accepting it proves extremely rewarding and worthwhile. It can help him solve most of his puzzles about Genesis and can lead him to understand why Genesis was recorded and preserved three millennia ago so that he, Ian Michael, can read it in the twenty-first century. (Hint: it was not preserved to tell him how old the earth is; there is no evidence that that was one of Moshe's concerns and no reason why it should have been).

Reading along with Moshe, we learn with him not how and when his world of sky and land had come into existence but *why*—which is far more important and valuable information. In the process, he learned who God was, what God did, and what God wanted for him. He also learned that his existence had ultimate meaning because it was a gift resulting from the will and action of a generous God who freely chose to bring him into being. It was a God who wanted him to exist and flourish and care for created reality (Gen. 2:15).

As he listened to Genesis, Moshe came to understand much about God's motivations and intentions, and about the general direction of Creation, by hearing words about God intermingled with words about the natural order. For Moshe this combination was not at all surprising; indeed, it was the way he had always thought about God and the rest of reality. It was the way all of Moshe's contemporaries thought. The narratives Moshe learned from childhood told of a God who had promised Moshe's ancestor Abraham, "I will make of you a great nation" (Gen. 12:2). Seeing that a human agent essential to the fulfillment—Leah—was rejected by her husband, *God opened her womb* (Gen. 29:31). This intermingling of words about God with words about what Ian Michael regards as "the natural order" was not surprising or jarring, nor did it seem in any way inappropriate to Moshe. It was, as Moshe had always understood, simply part of "what God does."

TIPTOEING INTO THE GENESIS-SCIENCE CONFLICT

That a face-value or literal reading of modern translations of the opening chapters of Genesis lies at the base of the Genesis-science conflict is now so widely understood that it seems foolish to question the matter and pointless to consider it further. Rather than exploring this conflict in more detail at this point, we will address it obliquely by retro-translating Genesis and thus producing an exhaustively literal English version of the ancient Hebrew text. We will translate every Hebrew word into English, and by comparing Scripture with Scripture, we will attempt to determine what each word and phrase originally meant. Employing this retro-translated Genesis, we are going to assume that a very similar text was what Moshe read or heard someone else read three thousand years ago and that his understanding of the text was a face-value (or compulsively literal) understanding. We are going to travel back in time to watch him experience the text.

At the same time—since we observers of these two readers can be in two imaginary places at once—we are going to look over Ian Michael's shoulder as he reads a modern, non-retro-translated Genesis—a version that appears to undergird some of his twenty-first-century (mis)undertandings. As we watch, we will concentrate on where and when differences show up between the respective readings by our two imaginary figures. (In our imaginary scenario, they cannot hear each other; but we can hear them both.) We will note where and how the two readings diverge, and we will explore what may lie behind the divergence. We want to know why Ian Michael's Genesis is so different from Moshe's. Listening along with Moshe to the Genesis story and looking over Ian Michael's shoulder as he reads will prove to be a surprisingly challenging enterprise. It will force us as observers to examine how we think about our own reading. This is very difficult to do but very much worthwhile.

Because the fundamental principle of retro-translation is to limit our understanding of the ideas and concepts expressed by the Hebrew text to those that Moshe himself could have conceived, he (as already noted) will be listening (in Hebrew) to something akin to our face-value, compulsively literal retro-translation of Genesis. Ian Michael is engrossed in the very same Genesis text, but he will most likely be reading the New International Version (NIV)—or, if he is really serious about exploring Genesis 1–11 and has had some guidance from his pastors or teachers, he may have the New Revised Standard Version (NRSV) in front of him. In any case, he will most likely be reading a version translated in the past quarter-century.

Close to three thousand years ago, somewhere in the Middle East, Moshe settled himself comfortably in the shade of a tree and watched as the community lector unrolled his Genesis scroll and began to read. We, too, will listen to that community reader, and at the same time, we will look over Ian Michael's shoulder as he opens his modern English translation to the first verses of Genesis.

Gen. 1:1. To begin with God brought into existence the **sky** and the **land** (OHV).	Gen. 1:1. In **the** beginning God created the **heavens** and the **earth** (NKJV).

Chapter Four

MOSHE'S TEXT AND IAN MICHAEL'S VERSIONS

In the process of translating Genesis, a definite article has appeared. The second word in almost all English versions of the Bible is the definite article *the*, preceding the noun *beginning*. This definite article is absent from all extant Hebrew manuscripts of Genesis as well as from the earliest translations, such as the Septuagint (translated in the second century BCE), and from many versions in other modern languages. Nowhere in any surviving Hebrew text of Genesis 1:1 does the word *ha* ("the") precede and introduce the noun *reshith* ("beginning"). Instead, the Hebrew text commences with the prefix *be-* ("in") to form the compound word bereshith ("in-beginning"). It is thus interesting that almost all English versions of Genesis 1:1 supply a definite article—"In *the* beginning." The few exceptions (such as

The Living Bible, the Common English Bible, and Robert Alter's translation) turn the first Hebrew sentence into a dependent clause: "When God began to create heaven and earth."

In the Koine Greek of the Septuagint, Genesis 1 begins with a construction curiously like and unlike the Hebrew text: "*En arche epoiesin ho theos*" (literally, "In beginning the God made"). Since a proper Koine Greek sentence could be composed without a definite article accompanying the word for "beginning" (*arche*), there was no reason for the Septuagint to include one.[1] At the same time, both in the Septuagint and in the New Testament, the Greek word for "God" (*theos*) sometimes takes a definite article and sometimes does not. The translators of the Vulgate, however, had no choice, because Latin has no definite article; translations from Latin must supply definite articles according to the practice of the receptor language. So the Vulgate text is not relevant here.

But starting with Wycliffe's Bible (a group of translations into Middle English that appeared under the direction of John Wycliffe from about 1382 to 1395), all English translations have included the definite article until very recently, where, as already noted, a few versions have paraphrased the Hebrew text by creating a dependent clause: "When God began to create." This, however, is a paraphrase rather than a strict translation; the Hebrew words do *not* constitute a dependent clause.

---

1. The familiar parallel wording in John 1:1 (also in Koine Greek) is similarly structured: *En arche en ho logos* ("In the beginning was the word"), perhaps as a deliberate echo of Gen. 1:1 (LXX). There is no Greek definite article with "beginning," but, again echoing Gen. 1:1, there is a definite article with "word." In English translations of John 1:1, the definite article is regularly included, as it is in Gen. 1:1 in Albert Pietersma and Benjamin G. Wright's *A New English Translation of the Septuagint* (New York: Oxford, 2007).

In his Early Modern English translation (1530, 1534), William Tyndale used the Greek and Hebrew texts of the New and Old Testaments as well as the Latin (Vulgate). Other notable Early Modern English versions included the Great Bible (1539), the first "authorized version"; the Geneva Bible (1560), the first English translation divided into verses; the Bishops' Bible (1568), which was Queen Elizabeth I's endeavor to create a new "authorized" version; and, of course, the King James Version (1611), which was long known as *the* authorized version (AV). All of these notable early versions include the definite article with the word *beginning*.

Perhaps, however, the absence of any definite articles in the Latin (Vulgate) text of the Hebrew Bible would have required subsequent English translators working from the Vulgate to insert definite articles according to their own semantic and stylistic judgment—influenced, of course, by the normal practices in English. Furthermore, even after Tyndale began the tradition of translating the Old Testament directly from the Hebrew text, the influence of earlier translations, including the Vulgate, continued to be strong. Therefore, unless there was a good reason to omit the definite article, there might well have been a continuing tendency to include it in the Bible's first (and rhetorically powerful) sentence. Thus the English reader of the Hebrew text—whether scholar, student, amateur, or translator—must use his or her best judgment. Complicating the matter is the fact that of the forty-nine occurrences of *reshith* with its various meanings—beginning, first, best, and so on—in the Hebrew Bible,[2] in no case is it preceded by the definite article.

---

2. Gen. 1:1; 10:10; 49:3; Exod. 23:19; 34:26; Lev. 2:12; 23:10b; Num. 15:20, 21; 18:12b; 24:20; Deut. 11:12; 18:4 (2×); 21:17; 26:2, 10; 1 Sam. 2:29; 15:21; 2 Chron. 31:5; Neh. 10:37; 12:44; Job 8:7; 40:19; 42:12; Pss. 78:51; 105:36; 111:10; Prov. 1:7; 3:9; 4:7; 8:22; 17:14; Eccl. 7:8; Isa. 46:10; Jer. 2:3; 26:1; 27:1; 28:1; 49:34, 35; Ezek. 20:40b; 44:30 (2×); 48:14b; Dan. 11:41; Amos 6:1, 6; Mic. 1:13b.

The question for us now is whether the presence or absence of *the* is significant. Or, more colloquially—so what? For some readers it may matter little whether or not the word *beginning* in the first verse of the Bible is preceded by the little word *the*. After all, people in the UK regularly say that someone is "in hospital," while Americans mean the same thing by saying "in *the* hospital." At the same time, Americans typically say that James is "away at college" but that Peter is "away at *the* university." It would seem foolish to make an issue out of a merely colloquial difference; and, indeed, in Genesis 1:1 it may well be nothing more than that.

But for other readers, it may, in fact, matter a great deal; for the initial Hebrew compound word *bereshith* (literally, "in-beginning") sets the tone for the rest of the first Creation narrative (Gen. 1:1–2:4a). The issue for Ian Michael—that is to say, for every modern reader of the Bible—is whether or not the narrative that follows should be regarded as an account of the absolute beginning of all material reality (as in the twenty-first century it is most often understood). One reason why it is understood in this way may be that *the* precedes *beginning*. In English, the presence of a definite article often emphasizes the importance of the following noun—in this case, *beginning*. Without the definite article, an English translation could be easily understood as indicating that the Hebrew narrator was simply informing Moshe (his intended audience) that an account of origins of the material things in which he was interested had now commenced. Whatever the intention of the translators, the presence of the definite article facilitates—though it certainly does not require—a more expansive interpretation.

BRINGING SPACE-TIME INTO EXISTENCE? OR NARRATING HOW MOSHE'S OWN WORLD BEGAN?

Here further questions arise, based on the general principles of retro-translation. Might the Hebrew author of Genesis 1 have deliberately omitted the definite article? Perhaps, but very probably not. The fact that there is not one Biblical example of the definite article with *reshith* suggests that the author was simply following the common linguistic practice.

At the same time, however, it seems even more unlikely that the inspired author intended to provide an account of the absolute origin of the entire universe (as Ian Michael understands the term, complete with the big bang theory). For in the next sentence the author noted that water and darkness were already present *prior to the events he was about to narrate*. Furthermore, his narrative implied that the combination of water and darkness was so potent and problematic that God took care of it in the very earliest stages of the Creation process. God introduced light on Day One and confined the water by means of a dome or vault (*raqia'*) on Day Two, before creating land, sea, and vegetation on Day Three. Furthermore, the emphasis of the narrative was (and is) not the *beginning* of the process but the *divine identity and loving generosity of its Originator*. To repeat: the Creation narrative, like the rest of Genesis 1–11, is *not science but theology*.

And what if the Genesis author was *not in fact describing the beginning of all material reality*? Modern science understands "material reality" to include not only planet Earth, the solar system, and the galaxy called the Milky Way but also a hundred million other galaxies, each containing a hundred million stars and probably as many planets. The author of Genesis 1 was evidently engaged in a very different and far more profound enterprise: telling Moshe and his contemporaries *why* their material reality (and yes, "the heavens and the earth" constituted all the material reality they knew) *existed at all.* In other words, perhaps the two Creation narratives (Gen. 1:1–2:4a and 2:4b–25) were for Moshe (and can be for Ian Michael) the answer to the three most fundamental human questions:

- Why is there something rather than nothing?
- What is the purpose and meaning of our existence—if indeed there is any purpose or meaning at all?
- How, then, should we live?

If the Creation narratives indeed were, and still are, intended to address these existential questions, the answer to the first question was and is, simply, "God": God's creative will is the ultimate answer to the puzzle of existence (Gen. 1:1). The answer to the second question was (and is) closely related: "Maximizing the potential of God's good creation—human, living, and material" (v. 28). And the answer to the third question logically followed (and still follows): "Actualizing God's infinite, universal, and unending love for the reality God has created."

After his initial topic sentence, the Genesis author *began* his profound theological narrative by describing a situation in which there was no individual "thing" and no specific "where"; invisible water and total darkness were "everything" and "everywhere." Far from saying that God created everything from nothing (literally in traditional Latin, *ex nihilo*, "out of nothing," an idea that emerged centuries later), the narratives explained to Moshe why the endless sky was over his head and the substantial land was under his feet. Perhaps Moshe took for granted the pre-Creation combination of water and darkness; the narrator provided no explanation for its existence; it just *was*, an actualization of utter formlessness, uselessness, and meaninglessness. God's first and second creative acts addressed the situation as God found it. With the darkness and the water taken care of, the stage was set for the appearance of Moshe's "dry land" (*yabbashah*, Gen. 1:9).

But how is Ian Michael supposed to know and understand this? Almost all the English translations of Genesis 1 that he can easily acquire refer to "*the* beginning." Not reading Hebrew, he may not give the matter a second thought, assuming that the Genesis narrator is answering his twenty-first-century scientific question—probably some version of, How did the universe originate? Or, if he remembers his high-school physics, he may formulate the question more scientifically: How did the space-time continuum come into existence?

So by the second word of the Genesis text in English, the conceptual path on which Ian Michael is encouraged to travel—by his KJV, NIV, NRSV, or any other translation he may have—has diverged from the retro-translated, OHV-identified path that Moshe was on. And all this by the time the first sentence of Genesis is barely underway. This divergence increases as we proceed from the second word of the NRSV to examine closely the eighth word.

"HEAVEN(S)" OR "SKY"?

In Ian Michael's NRSV the eighth word is "heavens," a translation of *shemayim*, the fifth word in the Hebrew text. Although in 1530 Tyndale translated *shemayim* with the singular form "heaven" (as Wycliffe's Bible had done about 150 years earlier), more than three-fourths of the English translations that followed have rendered it as plural: "heavens." This variation may have been encouraged by the fact that the Hebrew *shemayim* is neither singular nor plural but "dual," a syntactical form that has no English equivalent. Complicating the translator's task is the fact that in spite of its dual form, *shemayim* takes a singular verb—something like the English words *mathematics*, *physics*, *ethics*, and *gymnastics*, which, unlike *music*, are plural in form but nevertheless take singular verbs. So it is not surprising that *shemayim* is sometimes translated as "heaven," although more often as "heavens," perhaps to suggest the totality of astronomical realities rather than "the (singular) dwelling place of God." When Ian Michael turns to Psalm 19:1, for example, he reads, "The heavens are telling the glory of God," and that seems just right (partly because he has heard Haydn's choral masterpiece[3]).

But beyond the question of singular versus plural, another, more interesting question of translation arises. A perfectly appropriate and readily available English word would have largely avoided the problems of the translating the dual form *shemayim* as "heavens." That word is the unadorned English word for what Moshe saw every time he looked up: *sky*. Now *sky* doesn't take its plural form quite as grandly as does *heaven*, and even when pluralized (as in "O beautiful for spacious skies" in the patriotic hymn "America the Beautiful"), it is still tied to what Moshe regularly saw above him. Not so with *heavens*, which readily morphs into "starry heavens" and from there, with very little effort, into "galaxies" and on into "known universe."

Translators have rendered *shemayim* as "sky" quite often, obviously understanding it to be a perfectly legitimate English

---

3. Franz Joseph Haydn, "The Heavens Are Telling," in the oratorio *The Creation*, composed 1797–98.

equivalent. In Genesis 1–11 *shemayim* occurs twenty-two times, and NRSV translates it as "sky" nine (slightly more than 40 percent) of those times. When it refers to the dome created on the second day, NRSV has no difficulty identifying it as "sky" (Gen. 1:8). Similarly, when the waters are gathered together, the dry land appears "under the sky" (v. 9). God set the newly created lights in "the dome of the sky" (v. 17), and birds fly "across the dome of the sky" (v. 20); indeed, those birds are later identified as "birds of the sky."

But there is yet another plausible reason why translators probably decided that "heavens" was the most appropriate translation. Translating *shemayim* as "heavens" in verse 1 will probably (and understandably) lead Ian Michael to picture something immeasurably more vast than "sky." Perhaps the translators opted for the more expansive (and impressive) word *heavens* because the subject is Creation, and Creation is all about God and "the beginning." Did *shemayim* translated as "heavens" facilitate (perhaps unconsciously) a building-up of the narrative toward a grand, all-encompassing account of the way material reality came to be? Then again, are we perhaps seeing a pattern where, in fact, none exists? With this possibility hanging in the air we will proceed, moving in Ian Michael's NRSV translation from "the heavens" to "the earth."

MOSHE'S "LAND" DEVELOPED INTO IAN MICHAEL'S HOME PLANET

Much hangs on the way in which the eleventh word in Ian Michael's Bible is translated. The Hebrew word is *'erets*, rendered as either "land" or "earth." In the first nine chapters of Genesis (the narratives of Creation and Flood) it is overwhelmingly "earth"; in the remainder of the Hebrew

Bible it is overwhelmingly "land" or a "land-equivalent."[4] As we have already noted, given the availability of two acceptable English equivalents for a particular Hebrew word, starting with the KJV and continuing to the present, most translations of the early chapters of Genesis have opted for the more expansive and majestic option; and "earth" is a vastly larger and more impressive reality than "land" or "country" or "ground." This tendency is pivotal in this case, because a Creation story describing the coming into being of *'erets* almost instantaneously becomes a narrative of the origin of Ian Michael's home planet Earth and may even expand into the creation of the universe.

The consequences of the apparently simple choice to render *'erets* as "earth" rather than "land" ripple through the rest of the opening chapters of Genesis. Here, whenever 'erets occurs, it is translated as "earth" unless doing so would result in nonsense. For Ian Michael, reading that very first *'erets* translated as "earth" in the context where the first *shemayim* has already been translated "heavens" turns the rest of Genesis 1–11 into a *cosmological account of origins*.

Here we need to pause and explore what a "cosmological account" might have meant to Moshe since we already have a pretty good idea of what this language means to Ian Michael: To this twenty-first-century, intellectually curious Christian,

4. Early in Genesis, nine times out of ten, *'erets* has been translated as "earth." In the remainder of the Hebrew Bible it has been rendered as "earth" less than three times out of every ten occurrences (ratios have been rounded). Apparently, in the vast majority of the Hebrew Bible the translators have decided that "land" or a "land equivalent" such as "country" or "ground" is what the original authors intended. This penchant for rendering *'erets* as "earth" in Genesis 1–11 and not doing the same elsewhere is all the more unusual, for in every instance where *'erets* occurs, "land" or a "land equivalent" makes a meaningful English sentence. Why, then, is "earth" overwhelmingly preferred (9:1) here?

cosmology has to do with spherical bodies in mind-boggling numbers held in their respective orbits by gravity. These cosmological realities move at incredible speeds and are arranged in deep space as part of the larger accumulations known as galaxies.

Moshe, however, to the best of our knowledge, did not know any of this. He certainly did not know that he lived on a spherical planet, nor did he have a clue about universal gravitation that connected his planet to the "greater light." He knew of the land on which he lived, the sky-vault above it, and a "greater light" that moved over his land and across his sky—but that was all. Given Moshe's non-astronomical understanding of his reality, translating *'erets* as "earth" now seems to be so likely to mislead Ian Michael as to be not just a *poor* choice but a *wrong* choice—even though linguistically it remains a *possible* choice.

We have now arrived at the end of the first sentence of Genesis. Ian Michael is only a few seconds into his self-appointed task of understanding how he, a twenty-first-century Christian, should read—and not read—the Bible.

Gen 1:2. Now [as for] the **land** [it] was without form or function, **darkness** covered the ***tehom***, and God's spirit hovered over the surface of the **water** (OHV).	Gen 1:2. The **earth** was without form and void, and **darkness** was upon the face of **the deep**; and the Spirit of God was moving over the face of the **waters** (RSV).

Chapter Five

FOUR HEBREW WORDS: *'ERETS, YABBASHAH, TOV, YOM*

"Land," "Dry Ground," "Good," "Day"

Genesis 1:2 in the OHV retro-translation reads "land" for Moshe's *'erets*; Ian Michael's NRSV, NIV, and almost all other English versions read "earth." As we have seen, the two English words are both "correct" in the technical sense that both overlap with the semantic range of the Hebrew word. But in twenty-first-century English, there is a notable difference in connotation between "land" and "earth." During the development of the English language, the meaning of "land" has changed little, but the meaning of "earth" has expanded enormously. From being more or less a synonym for "land" as Moshe understood *'erets*, "earth" has become, far more often than not, the planet on which Ian Michael and his more than 7.6 billion current contemporaries exist in widely varying degrees of prosperity, comfort, and satisfaction.

Unfortunately modern English translators of Genesis 1–11 have regularly chosen "earth" for *'erets* rather than "land," but that would certainly not have been the choice of the Genesis storyteller if he or she had been thinking, speaking, or writing in modern English. A moment's reflection reveals that for Moshe to understand and communicate the storyteller's meaning, the choice would have to have been "land." The word *'erets* might have meant "rich dark soil," but that would still have been a form of (and very similar in meaning to) "land." What *'erets* clearly could not have meant for Moshe is what Ian Michael almost certainly takes "earth" to mean: the spherical entity in space (and more specifically in the solar system) on which he lives.

The very next time *'erets* occurs in the text (Gen. 1:10), it is often translated into English as "land," particularly in more recent versions,[1] for the simple reason that it parallels *yabbashah* ("dry ground"). Recent translators have evidently resisted making "dry ground" synonymous with the whole planet. If *'erets* had been understood, and therefore translated, as "land" in verses 1 and 2, where it clearly refers to the same reality as in verse 10, it is much more likely that Ian Michael would still be reading the same Creation story that Moshe read by the time both reached verse 10.

A straightforward and consistent rendering of *'erets* as "land" in English translations through the last several hundred years would have spared Ian Michael many fruitless intellectual battles. Consider, for instance, the idea, warmly received in some

1. In addition to NIV, see, for example, the Contemporary English Version (CEV), New English Translation (NET), International Standard Version (ISV), New Living Translation (NLT), and Tree of Life Version (TLV).

conservative Protestant quarters, that perhaps the planet Earth as a rocky, water-enshrouded sphere, having been brought into existence by God according to Genesis 1:1, circled the sun for eons before Creation proper got underway (v. 3). This proposal is sometimes called the gap theory because it postulates two Creation events separated by an indefinite amount of time. If, during the interim, God is envisioned as engaged in further creative activity, it is regarded as an "active gap"; if not, it is considered a "passive gap." This gap theory has been thought necessary because some rocks on Earth measure billions of years old according to radioactive dating techniques, and they need to be taken into account. Additionally, starlight that has been traveling across the universe at the speed of light for billions of years is now visible from Earth; how that can be is one of the conundrums faced by all who translate *'erets* as "earth"—meaning Earth—rather than "land."

Those who espouse a gap theory assume that Genesis 1:1, 2 refers to the planet Ian Michael knows as Earth. But it is unnecessary to propose a gap theory if Genesis 1 is not, in fact, talking about planet Earth in verses 1 and 2 but is instead referring to Moshe's familiar "land." Furthermore, the principle that Scripture should be allowed to interpret itself would seem to eliminate the gap theory as even a remote possibility, since there is no Biblical evidence that planetary bodies (as distinct from stars) could have been conceptualized when Genesis 1:1–2:4a was composed. The evidence in the passage itself (and that is all the evidence there is) stipulates that Moshe's "land" was "dry ground" (*yabbashah*, Gen. 1:10) and thus could not conceivably have been a water-covered planet (or protoplanet) circling the sun for eons. This misunderstanding, however, is the unfortunate result of translating *'erets* as "earth" instead of "land" in Genesis 1:1, 2 and equating it with *yabbashah* in verse 10 as most versions still do. In a situation like this, a translator's sense of what is culturally, and therefore linguistically, "right and proper" can exert immense influence, for better or worse—outweighing even the evidence of the actual text being translated. In this specific case, it has been hugely influential for generations.

PRE-CREATION WATER AND DARKNESS

According to Genesis 1, darkness enveloped the water, the only existing material reality, before Creation began. The narrative simply noted its presence, providing Moshe no information about its coming into being, so he could well have assumed, without thinking further about it, that it had always existed. He was, of course, not listening to a *scientific description* of Creation (such accounts were still 2,500 years in the future); he was listening to a *theological explanation* of the reality he knew as a matter of "what God does." He knew that God could do anything imaginable, so he had no problem with the idea of pre-Creation water and darkness. Listening to the theological narrative, he wanted the explanation to proceed. Having heard the story before, he knew that his sky and land were in the offing, and he was eager to hear it again.

Ian Michael, on the other hand, is culturally conditioned to be scientifically curious; he has a lot of questions, and he wants answers. For example: Since visible light is a form of radiation, does the Creation narrative mean that there was no radiation of any kind before God said, "Let there be light"? Where did Creation take place? It must have been somewhere in the known universe, since there wasn't any other "where"—in deep space, perhaps? Since the "waters" are described as having a "face," a surface, and to have had a surface, there must have been a surrounding atmosphere, even though it is not mentioned. Otherwise, how could there have been a "surface"? Why isn't air mentioned along with the darkness and the water?

These are all good, thoughtful questions; but they are Ian Michael's questions, coming from Ian Michael's world. The Genesis narrative, coming from Moshe's very different world, and being a *theological* story with a very different motivation, does not (and could not be expected to) answer them. A proper retro-translation of Genesis ensures that no realities or concepts that Moshe could not have imagined are introduced into Ian Michael's English version of the story. That being the case, Ian Michael is certainly not going to get answers to his modern scientific questions from the ancient theological narrative that Moshe heard, understood, cherished, and preserved. If Ian Michael *seems* to get answers to these or similar questions from a modern Bible translation,[2] he should view that translation with great skepticism. He should close it and put it back on the shelf where he found it.

MOSHE'S THREATENING *TEHOM*: A REALITY IAN MICHAEL CANNOT COMPREHEND

The *tehom*—variously rendered as "the Abyss," "Sheol," or "the Deep"—was where Creation had to begin, since it, along with darkness (which is itself literally *nothing*, being only the *absence* of light) was everywhere and everything, as the curtain rose and the narrator began to answer Moshe's persistent existential questions: Where did everything come from? Why is what is here, including me, here? What, if anything, does all this mean for me and my existence? Why should I care?

2. The Good News Translation (GNT, 1992) and the International Standard Version (ISV, 1995) translate Genesis 1:1 as "In the beginning God created the universe."

In some sense, Moshe's existence was always threatened by the possibility that God might not have fully subdued the *tehom* at Creation, so if Moshe was able to go far enough beneath the *land* on which he existed or above the vault (*raqia'*) overhead, he might still come face-to-face with that dreaded reality. After all, it had broken loose once before: it had escaped from its God-wrought bonds at the time of the Great Flood. If God had not "remembered" (Gen. 8:1) and intervened, the resurgent *tehom* might have terminated everything, even Noah's existence. But for God's intervention on that occasion in the dim and distant past, the tehom would have also destroyed forever Moshe's beloved *'erets*.

The *tehom* was not, however, always seen in Scripture as fearsome. As long as God kept it tethered, it could be viewed as a potential source of blessing: the Almighty

will bless you
with blessings of heaven above,
blessings of the deep [*tehom*] that lies beneath,
blessings of the breasts and of the womb.
(Gen. 49:25)

"GOOD" AS AN ACTIVE ATTRIBUTE

A perfectly reasonable question is sometimes asked by elementary school students when, in a Bible class, they are told that God created light and then said that it was "good" (Gen. 1:3, 4): "If the light was good, was the darkness bad?" The harried teacher replies with something like, "Well, sort of, maybe, perhaps. I think it's time for recess." If the teacher had been able to read the Hebrew that underlies the word *good* in English translations, matters might have been different.

Here the word *good*, although close to the Hebrew word *tov*, doesn't have quite the same semantic range and therefore doesn't have precisely the same meaning. But that is not the whole story, because *good*, standing on its own, often does mean the opposite of *bad*. But when *good* is part of the three-word sequence *good*, *better*, *best*, it means something that is OK, acceptable—not something that is the opposite of *bad*. In addition, it can imply that there are other things quite superior. Neither of these meanings of *good*, however, catches the exact sense of *tov* in the theological narrative of Creation. Here God reversed, corralled, and controlled the pre-Creation darkness and *tehom*. Then light was functional: it performed a worthwhile task; it achieved a useful end; it was *good for something*. In short, it *worked*. It was *tov*.

This functional aspect of being "*good for* [something]" can be, of course, recaptured in English, as we just did. But clarifying the meaning in this way requires additional English words that would make Ian Michael's version seem more like a paraphrase than an actual translation. So most English versions have rendered the Hebrew *tov* simply as "good." Believing that Moshe would have appreciated the functional, *good-for-something* aspect of *tov*, we have retro-translated it here as "functioned well." In other words, it accomplished its purpose. It *worked*. It was *good for* dispelling the pre-Creation darkness that had to be eliminated so that Creation could proceed.

UNCREATED DARKNESS AS A CONTINUING ASPECT OF CREATED REALITY

The Creation days (and what occurred on each) constitute the substance of the first theological explanation of Creation (Gen. 1:1–2:4a). Not so, however, for the Creation nights.

The pre-Creation darkness was named "night," but nowhere in the Genesis narrative did Moshe hear of God *creating night* as, by bringing light, God *created day*.

This concept is very difficult for Ian Michael to comprehend, for he knows day and night as correlative and complementary entities that cannot be understood separately. "Day" implies "night," and "night" presupposes "day." They are both the effects of a rotating spherical earth in relation to a fixed sun. Given this astronomical geometry, the sun's light can illuminate only one half of the spherical earth's surface at any moment; the other half is necessarily *un*illuminated. Furthermore, the rotating Earth has approximately equal periods of light and darkness. Ian Michael knows all this without even thinking about it. Moshe, on the other hand, saw no reason why the night could not be a great deal longer or shorter than the day. How the sun managed to get from the western point of sunset to the eastern point of sunrise puzzled Moshe as it did all of his contemporaries. He had no reason to suppose it would take the same length of time as did the westward journey across the sky from sunrise to sunset.

It is hard for Ian Michael to imagine himself living on Moshe's beloved "land"—that is, land *that did not move*, land that was illuminated and made fertile by "the greater light" (Gen., 1:16) that traveled across the sky daily from east to west. Pre-Creation darkness returned each night as the sun, now invisible, made its recurring trek from west to east—under the *'erets* or, perhaps, through it, since "foundations of the earth" were in the way. Moshe did not like darkness; he feared it with an almost visceral dread; it was a symbol of pre-Creation darkness, of *un*reality. That fear persisted long after Moshe's time; indeed, it was still an issue for the early followers of Jesus. For them, one of the most attractive features of the New Jerusalem was that "there will be no more night; . . . for the Lord God will be their light" (Rev. 22:5).

Each of the Creation days was explicitly defined as consisting of *daylight*, and each daylight-day was separated from its predecessor and its successor by a night of pre-Creation darkness. Nowhere in the narrative is there any indication of the twenty-four-hour "Creation day" that Ian Michael takes for granted, having heard about it since childhood. He naturally assumes that it is the same sort of twenty-four-hour day he has experienced all his life, and he seldom if ever notices that his idea of a twenty-four-hour day completely disregards the Genesis definition of "day" as a "daylight day": "God called the light Day, and the darkness he called Night" (Gen. 1:5). A Creation day was not twenty-four hours long—nor was it indefinitely long. The Genesis author clearly identified which of the various possible meanings of *day* was intended, explicitly limiting the meaning of *yom* to the daylight. So *yom* could not plausibly have been extended to twenty-four hours, much less have meant eons of time. (Moshe would have scratched his head at *eons*.)

Ian Michael has not yet finished reading Genesis 1:4, but because of the choices translators have more-or-less consistently made when rendering *'erets* ("land"), *shemayim* ("sky"), *tov* ("good"), and *yom* ("day"), the narrative that Ian Michael reads is significantly different from the narrative that Moshe heard. Moshe's OHV narrative described something that was peculiar indeed. It was a "day" defined by "there was evening and there was morning" (vv. 5b, 8b, 13, 19, 23, 31b). If these are to be understood as the limits of the reality being described, it is not a day at all; it is clearly a night. What this puzzling entity might have been is explored in the next chapter.

Gen 1: 5. There was **evening**, then **dawning**—One [Creation] Day (OHV).	Gen 1:5. And the **evening** and the **morning** were the first day (KJV).

Chapter Six

THE CONUNDRUM OF AN "EVENING-MORNING" DAY

Do érev *("Evening") and* boqer *("Morning") Express Concepts That Are No Longer Useful?*

We believe Moshe heard Genesis very much as we have rendered it in retro-translation (OHV); at least, this is the closest we can come to reconstructing what he heard. An essential principle of retro-translation is that if something is defined by the author of the Hebrew narrative, then that is the definition of that reality *in the narrative*. Thus, because the Hebrew "day" (*yom*) is defined as a daylight-day (Gen. 1:5), that definition remains the working definition of "day" in the retro-translated text unless and until the author changes the definition.

So what do we now have in verse 5b, "There was evening and there was dawning, one day" (OHV)? Has the author abruptly changed the definition of "day" from "daylight-day" to "night-dark-plus-daylight-day"? Not likely. But as the Hebrew text has been traditionally translated in, for example, KJV, "The evening and the morning were the first day," the author defines "day" as daylight, but then, without pausing to draw a breath, replaces that definition with another: "The evening and the morning were the first day."

It could hardly be clearer. The first "day" (as KJV delineates it) now consisted of darkness (evening) and light (morning). And this comes immediately after "day" had been defined—by God, no less—as a period of time defined by "light." How can this be?

Moshe's Hebrew words for "evening" and "morning" were, respectively, *'erev* and *boqer*, and in the text each is accompanied by a form of the verb "to be" (*hayah*). Thus the most literally accurate English rendering of the Hebrew sentence is, "There was evening, and there was dawning, one day."[1] Biblical translators and exegetes have long puzzled over what the Hebrew language here actually meant, and thus should still mean. All agree that it is difficult to now determine the narrator's intent, and for several reasons.

First, since the text evidently describes an aspect or attribute of "one day," it is curious (and perhaps significant) that the author mentions "evening" before "morning" rather than the other way around. Morning usually comes before evening in a description of a day, and certainly if the day is understood as a "daylight-day," since the coming of light

---

1. Unfortunately NRSV uses the ordinal rather than the cardinal form of the number ("the first day," rather than "one day" as specified in the Hebrew text), probably to conform to the ordinal form in the Hebrew for the second through the sixth days (Gen. 1:8, 13, 19, 23, 31).

would begin the day. In the ancient Biblical world, as in the modern Western world, that the day began in the morning[2] and ended in the evening[3] was taken for granted. Second, if *yom* is a "daylight day" characterized and defined by "light," it seems odd that the author immediately changed the definition of "day" to include evening and thus darkness.

Third, it is notable that the description of the seventh day, God's Sabbath, did not conclude with a similar summary statement, "There was evening and there was morning, a seventh day." Perhaps this change reflects the fact that the Sabbath was not a day of divine activity but a day of divine rest (Gen. 2:3). On the other hand, Ian Michael, with his penchant for scientific precision, may be puzzled by Genesis 2:1, 2: "Thus the heavens and the earth were finished, and all their multitude. And on the seventh day God finished the work that he had done, and he rested on the seventh day from

2. In support of the day beginning in the morning in early Old Testament times, Jacob Milgrom cites Gen. 1:5; 19:33, 34; Lev. 7:15; 22:30; Num. 9:11; 33:3; Josh. 5:10; Judg. 19:4–9; 1 Sam. 19:11; 28:18, 19. *Leviticus 23–27: A New Translation with Introduction and Commentary*, Anchor Bible Commentaries 3B (New York: Doubleday, 2001), 1967.

3. The "sabbath" (*sic*) instituted in Lev. 23:32 is one of the most notable twenty-four-hour time periods in the Hebrew Bible. Interestingly, this twenty-four-hour period is not identified as a *yom* in Hebrew, although it is so identified (as a "day") in English Bible versions. "It is to be a sabbath of complete rest to you, and you shall humble your souls; on the ninth of the month at evening, from evening until evening you shall keep your sabbath" (NASB). Here the Israelites were instructed to reverence the annual Day of Atonement by beginning the celebration with what was evidently a lead-in period of twelve hours of preparation that included fasting. This lead-in is never attached to the weekly (seventh-day) Sabbath in the entire Hebrew Bible. However, following the return from captivity, devout Jews began the practice in order to "guard the edges of the Sabbath" (Neh. 13:19). Observing the weekly Sabbath from sundown on the sixth day to sundown on the seventh day was the practice of Jesus and the Jews of His time. This continues to be the practice of observant Jews to the present.

all the work that he had done." Ian Michael may well ask in some frustration, "Was Creation finished on the sixth day or the seventh day? Which was it?"

THE ONGOING CHALLENGE OF TRANSLATION

Is there any way in which the translators of the Bible can choose words that make it immediately and perfectly clear to Ian Michael just what the Hebrew text said to Moshe? Unfortunately, that is not really possible. For example, the concept of a difference in kind, in elemental substance, between day and night no longer exists. As a result, there is now no need to demarcate the limits of the created "light" to clearly differentiate it from the pre-Creation darkness. With no need to express this particular distinction, there are no English words to do so. It has become a *former* need, which no longer exists. Ian Michael is completely stymied, and it is a mark of intellectual maturity for him to recognize that there are some things in the past that he just cannot understand—just as there are some things in professional music or philosophy that a computer scientist *as a computer scientist* may not be able to comprehend or does not need to understand.

Ian Michael may be stymied, but he need not be totally frustrated. As the Earth (not *'erets*) rotates, the portion of its ever-advancing surface exposed to the light of the sun transitions from day into night at a theoretical line called *the terminator*[4]. Viewed (conceptually) from space, this is the line between light and darkness that moves from east to west as the Earth rotates underneath the observer. Perhaps it could be explained to Ian Michael that the moment the day-night

4. A "terminator," or "twilight zone," is a moving line that distinguishes the illuminated (day) side from the dark (night) side of a planetary body.

terminator passed by, that instant, that moment in time, was something like (but certainly not identical to) the feeling the Hebrew *'erev* evoked in Moshe's consciousness.

We have encountered many instances in which Ian Michael has concepts—and words to express these concepts—that Moshe could not have understood simply because they were not understood by any human until centuries, sometimes millennia, later. Apogee and perigee, the "high" and "low" points of a satellite's orbit around the Earth, may be a useful pair of examples. The Hebrews did not know of the planet we call Earth, of the omnipresent force that Ian Michael knows as gravity, or of planetary satellites. Since it is gravity that holds the satellites in orbit, and Moshe knew nothing about gravity, he could not think of apogee and perigee. And, of course, he did not have any words to express a thought that he could not think. Here, however (and significantly), the shoe is on the other foot: *'erev* is an idea that Moshe could easily conceive but that Ian Michael can imagine only after going through mental gymnastics and for which he has no single word. If he is to put himself in Moshe's world at all, he has to substitute for Moshe's simple *'erev* something like the complicated and still inadequate phrase, "the moment when the day-night terminator passes by." The closest descriptor we can come up with is "sunset."

BACK TO *'EREV* AND *BOQER*

So why the unusual language, "And there was evening [*'erev*, "dusk"] and there was morning [*boqer*, "dawn"]" (Gen. 1:5b, 8b, 13, 19, 23, 31b)? What purpose was served by repeating this puzzling Hebrew language six times in a description of a seven-day Creation? Our best answer is that if the Genesis author's definition of "day" was to play its critically important role in this Creation narrative, then its limits—its beginning and its ending—needed to be clearly stated. And this is what the author proceeded to do. "There was *'erev* [sunset]" defined the end of Creation Day One, and "there was *boqer* [sunrise]" marked the beginning of the second. In between these two moments, pre-Creation darkness returned for a while; but, not being part of God's Creation, it passed without mention. It was, after all, seven *days* that made up Creation *week*—just as for modern Americans "a week's work" is not 168 (7 times 24) hours, but more like 40 (5 times 8) hours. If one understands the linguistic practice, there is no puzzle, much less a problem.

Still, as Moshe listened to the narrative of Genesis and mentally relived the events it described, he was reminded that, yes, periods of time elapsed between the Creation days; but they were unimportant. Because they were not part of Creation, there was no need for them in the Creation narrative. And because they were not part of the narrative, there was no meaningful time within them. Nothing was accomplished between the end of one Creation day and the beginning of the next. In that sense they did not even exist; they were "nothings"—even less significant than the nights of the modern American "work week."

Thus Moshe, unlike Ian Michael, had no problem with the idea of God "finishing" the work of Creation on Sabbath, because that was the earliest possible time in the Creation narrative when the events of the preceding six days could be pronounced "completed." Similarly, the first possible occasion when the events of Creation Day One could be summed up was immediately after the first *boqer* had restarted the Creation narrative for both the author and his audience (Moshe). The first actual *boqer* was on Creation Day Two, because God's origination of light on the previous day had marked the beginning of the whole Creation process.

So as Moshe heard the theological explanation, Creation Day One began with the coming of light at God's command and ended with 'erev ("dusk" or "sunset"). This was the first of the six occurrences of 'erev in the Creation narrative; thus the final 'erev at the end of Creation Day Six was at the very place it needed to be in the Creation narrative to usher in the Sabbath, God's rest.

It made sense to Moshe, and he was satisfied. Now it can make sense to Ian Michael, and he too can be satisfied.

Gen 1:6–8. God said, "Let there be a **vault** within the water, and let it separate the water." God made the **vault** and separated the water under the **vault** from the water above the vault, and thus it came to be. God named the **vault** "**sky**." And there was evening then dawning—**a** second Creation day (OHV).

Gen 1:6–8. And God said, "Let there be a **dome** in the midst of the waters, and let it separate the waters from the waters." So God made the **dome** and separated the waters that were under the **dome** from the waters that were above the **dome**. And it was so. God called the **dome** **Sky**. And there was evening and there was morning, **the** second day (NRSV).

Chapter Seven

IF "FIRMAMENT" IS MEANINGLESS AND "EXPANSE" IS MISLEADING, WHAT WAS THE *RAQIA'*?

The Vault/Dome Is Important

In Genesis 1:6–8, Ian Michael's NRSV is very similar to Moshe's OHV. The word *firmament* has, of course, disappeared from Ian Michael's Bible—and good riddance. *Firmament* never properly reflected the language and message of Moshe's Hebrew scrolls, where the word was *raqia'*. Ian

Michael, like the myriad Bible readers during the past several centuries, has had only a very hazy conception of what a "*firmament*" actually was (or is, or might be). How would you know one if you saw it? The absence of firmament from almost all modern translations does not bother Ian Michael because he never knew what the word meant anyway.

However, the disappearance of *firmament* has left in its place a problem. As now translated in modern versions, the Hebrew *raqia'* apparently identified either something solid and structured (such as a dome or vault) or, alternatively, something ethereal and diaphanous (such as an expanse or space). A sky-associated dome, presumably a hemispherical structure viewed from outside, or a sky-associated vault, a similar structure viewed from inside, is something that Ian Michael can understand easily enough, but he knows (on the basis of overwhelming empirical evidence) that such an entity does not now exist. How then could the author of Genesis have described it as established by God on Creation Day Two? It was not introduced as something that needed further explanatory details to justify its existence. In fact, it was introduced into the narrative as if it were a normal, functional, necessary, and recognized reality—something that would be expected to appear at precisely that point in the narrative.

Whatever it was, the role of *raqia'* in the Creation narrative marks it as important: it was the first material reality that God created. One way to judge its significance is to note how many times it is mentioned. As a criterion of importance this is admittedly arguable, for there are many reasons why a particular element in a story might be mentioned often. Still, we should not ignore the fact that in fifteen verses (Gen. 1:6–20) the *raqia'* is specifically named *nine* times. So what can Ian Michael possibly make of a reality that doesn't now exist but was so important that portions of the Creation narrative appear to hinge on it being introduced at this point in the narrative of Creation? Considerations like these have facilitated the translation of the ancient Hebrew *raqia'* by modern Western words like "space" and "expanse."

It comes as no surprise that translators through the centuries have tried to help. In the late fourth century the Latin Vulgate, largely the work of Saint Jerome, translated *raqia'* as *firmamentum*, and a millennium later, toward the end of the fourteenth century, Wycliffe's Bible (translated from the Vulgate) introduced the Anglicized word *firmament*. When William Tyndale translated the Hebrew Bible directly into English in 1530, he adopted "firmament" as the translation of *raqia'*, and for more than five hundred years that remained the consistent practice of English translators. The Latin word was simply given an English form (by dropping its Latin neuter singular ending). This was how *firmament* came into the English Bible.

The appellation *firmament* did not, however, solve the problem of what exactly the word identified; instead, it camouflaged the problem. Few English-speaking readers have had any idea of what, if anything, the word actually means. Thus, assuming that it must mean *something* (it is, after all, right here at the beginning of God's Word), they have failed to suspect a serious disconnection between what Moshe understood to have happened on Creation Day Two and what Ian Michael envisions on hearing the word *firmament*. In fact, Ian Michael usually pictures nothing at all, because he has no idea that *firmament* is an Anglicized form of an old Latin word that once upon a time referred to something solid and *firm*. This linguistic fact, however, provides little if any help, particularly if the recent alternative translations of *raqia'* as "space" or "expanse" are in any way correct; the idea of a "firm space or expanse" seems simply incoherent.

In contrast, Moshe had no problems with the idea of *raqia'*. He had a clear mental image of a *raqia'* as a vault or dome and understood why it preceded the other material objects that God created. He realized that God, who had begun Creation in the midst of water and darkness everywhere, had by means of a *raqia'* divided the water into that above the *raqia'* and that below it (Gen. 1:7), thereby making space in the middle for Moshe's land (*'erets*). Ian Michael, however, not at all sure what in the world a "firmament" might have been, and even less clear about how it could be useful in interplanetary space, does not realize that a water-everywhere problem existed at the beginning of Creation (he has already forgotten about the frightening *tehom*). Not recognizing the problem, he invests little effort in figuring out how God could have solved it. Thus for Ian Michael, Creation Day Two is essentially meaningless. Nothing much happened, and whatever did happen was not declared "good" (that is, effectively functional); so why worry about exactly what it might have been?

IF THE "FIRMAMENT" IS REAL, HOW "FIRM" IS IT?

Recognizing that the word *firmament* has been virtually unintelligible to the majority of Bible readers, translators in the past few decades have searched for a modern English word or phrase that captures the meaning that *raqia'* evidently had for Moshe. That ancient meaning, they knew, derived from, and was therefore closely related to, the verb *raqa'*, which meant "to beat out" or "to shape by beating." In the Hebrew Bible, this verb typically (though not always) refers to the beating out and shaping of metal. How then are the translators supposed to communicate the idea of a "beaten-out" dome or vault that Moshe took for granted as overarching his land—and do so in a way that is intelligible to Ian Michael, who knows for sure that such an entity doesn't exist in the outer space that surrounds his planet Earth—and never did?

Two possibilities are available to translators, and both have been tried. Translators following the first option render *raqia'* as "dome" or "vault" and leave the matter there for exegetes and homilists to address as best they can. Those taking the second option translate *raqia'* as "expanse" or "space" on the grounds that "beating out" something expands its surface area. Furthermore, two Hebrew passages refer to "stretching out" the heavens like a tent (Ps. 104:2; Isa. 40:22), and while obviously metaphorical, these might permit some similarity of meaning between *heavens* and *expanse*. (Similarly metaphorical but on the *dome* or *vault* side are the references to skies made firm in Proverbs 8:28 and hard as a molten mirror in Job 37:18.) Not surprisingly, when Ian Michael reads *expanse*, he thinks of "atmospheric expanse," which certainly does exist, so this translation is understandable and fits with what he knows about his home planet.

As the English word *firmament* began to fall from translators' favor in the mid-twentieth century, Bible versions with *dome* or *vault* appeared as well as versions with *expanse* or *space*. Of the latter, one of the earliest was a retranslation of the Torah from the Jewish Publication Society (1962), followed by the New American Standard Bible (NASB, 1971), the New International Version (NIV, 1984), and others. But the idea that *raqia'* could possibly be rendered as "expanse" was not entirely new. Young's Literal Translation (YLT, 1864) had raised the possibility a century earlier, but most of his contemporaries did not follow Robert Young's lead; translators of that time were evidently content with *firmament*.

In Moshe's understanding of reality, a firm, substantial dome or vault was essential to the preservation of his existence. He knew from the Genesis theological narrative that God had produced a *raqia‘* on Creation Day Two in order to keep the threatening *tehom* safely confined and thus to ensure the continuance of his beloved land. But we have not yet solved the problem of the word (and reality) *firmament*. Because it so clearly illustrates the Bible translators' dilemma and because its translation affects the way in which the narrative of Genesis 1–11 is understood, we will return to the topic of the firmament in chapter 12.

A LIGHT IN A "SKY-VAULT," NOT A NUCLEAR-FUELED STAR

It is often noted that the terminology of "the greater light" and "the lesser light" was employed by the author of Genesis in order to avoid using the specific designations of these astronomical bodies. This aversion was entirely appropriate because the Hebrew words for sun and moon were also the names of ancient pagan deities, and the author wanted to remind his hearers that there was only one God, YHWH, the One Who Ever Is, and Who Is the Source of All Reality.[1]

But if Ian Michael stops there, he misses something very important. As Moshe listened, he pictured the sun rising in the east and, because it had been set in the vault, moving across the daytime sky as the vault rotated from east to west over his head. As it did so, it "lit up the land" and marked off the days of high ceremony that structured Moshe's year. Getting the sun from setting in the west back under his land to rise in the east was something God did and was thus part of Moshe's theological understanding. The "greater light" was simply being moved by the Creator.

1. The sacred personal name *Yahweh*, never pronounced by practicing Jews even when reading Scripture, was evidently derived from the verb *hayah*, "to be," and incorporated the ideas of Being Itself (or, more colloquially, "Ultimate Is-ness") and hence the Eternal Source of All Reality.

The facility with which Ian Michael mentally substitutes "sun" for "greater light" often lulls him into assuming that his sun is conceptually identical to Moshe's "greater light." But this is far from the truth of the matter. For Ian Michael knows the sun as a relatively large and vitally important cosmological entity: it is huge compared to the earth, and its apparently diminutive size to the naked eye is the result of its distance from planet Earth. He knows that the sun is not "set" in any "dome" and that it does not actually "pass" overhead; its apparent movement from east to west is the result of Earth turning, not of the sun actually changing its spatial relation to Earth. He knows that the sun is the parent star of the solar system and that Earth circles around it, making one complete rotation every 365 and a quarter days while at the same time revolving on its own axis every twenty-four hours. Ian Michael takes all of this for granted whenever he hears the word *sun*. And every bit of this knowledge is solidly and squarely in the realm of *nature*, while all of Moshe's much more limited knowledge of his environment was solidly and squarely in the realm of *theology*, all part of "what God did." So Moshe's "greater light" is not the same as Ian Michael's sun—not even close.

The more deeply Ian Michael recognizes the difference between his own *natural* and *scientific* "sun" and Moshe's *theological* "greater light," the easier it will be for him to realize that science and theology are not enemies, as often supposed, but, in fact, allies in the ongoing human endeavor to understand both the *facts* and the *meaning* of existence. To be sure, the two projects differ greatly in subject matter and methodology, but they are both motivated by profound intellectual curiosity and desire to understand the reality (and Reality) in which we live. This is truly *good news*.

Gen 6:6, 7. And Yahweh was sorry that he had made humankind upon the **land**, and it pained his heart. So Yahweh said, "I will eliminate from the **land** the human beings I have created" (OHV).

Gen 6:6, 7. And the Lord was sorry that he had made humankind upon the **earth**, and it grieved him to his heart. So the Lord said, "I will blot out from the **earth** the human beings I have created" (NRSV).

Chapter Eight

THE GREAT FLOOD IS A CHALLENGE LINGUISTICALLY AND HYDROLOGICALLY

Did the Flood Cover the "Earth" or the "Land"?

Very early in the narrative of the Great Flood, it is made clear that God was entirely and solely responsible for that epochal event. God took full credit; it was (and is) obvious that humans, no matter how violent, were utterly incapable of bringing that kind of total disaster upon the *'erets.* It involved setting in motion unimaginable forces that acted upon huge entities; the whole event was beyond anything that humans could possibly accomplish. In a conceptual world with only two kinds of explanation—human and divine—whatever humans could not accomplish, God did. Period. Thus God necessarily took full responsibility. But for what, exactly? Did the Flood cover the entire planet? Or was it all of the land that Moshe was familiar with, had heard about, or was able to imagine?

At this point the Hebrew-to-English translators' historically conditioned sense of the "right and proper" meaning of the Hebrew text takes on crucial significance. Here their image of a "Flood of Biblical proportions" becomes determinative for Ian Michael's understanding of the nature and extent of the Flood (since he has little if any direct access to the original Hebrew narrative). Beginning at least as far back as William Tyndale's Old Testament (1530), the word *'erets* has been consistently translated as "earth" wherever possible in the narrative of the Flood, and that is clearly a reasonable possibility regarding the extent of the Great Flood. So Ian Michael almost always understands it as having covered planet Earth—in spite of a host of unanswered scientific and common-sense questions, such as, Where did the water come from, and where did it go?

Thus the narrative is usually, for Ian Michael, a description of an unimaginable natural catastrophe overwhelming a planet that Moshe knew nothing about, rather than a swamping of Moshe's homeland (*'erets*) by a *tehom* that was released from its God-established confinement and was out of control once again. That confinement had been accomplished

Genesis 7:3, 4. "and seven pairs of the birds of the air also, male and female to keep their kind alive on the face of all the **land**. For in seven days . . . every living thing that I have made I will erase from the face of the **ground**." (OHV).

Genesis 7:3, 4. "and seven pairs of the birds of the air also, male and female, to keep their kind alive on the face of all the **earth**. For in seven days . . . every living thing that I have made I will blot out from the face of the **ground**." (NRSV).

by the second day of Creation and was an essential part of the process by which Moshe's "land" was brought into existence by the Creator God whom Moshe worshipped.

Such is the power of a translation to transform the meaning of a sacred text.

"LAND," "EARTH," AND "THE FACE OF [NOAH'S] GROUND"

According to the narrative, having taken responsibility for bringing a Flood upon the *'erets*, God foretold how far the Flood would extend and described it in such a way that a careful reader can at least partially determine what it would cover. Ancient Hebrews often emphasized by repetition: an idea presented in one sentence was often followed by the same idea expressed in slightly different words—a rhetorical strategy known as synonymous parallelism. In this instance (Gen. 7:3, 4), God described the extent of the Flood as covering "the face of all the earth [*'erets*]," and then reinforced it in slightly different words, "the face of the ground [*adamah*]." Earlier in the narrative (Gen. 2:7), God had created from "the dust of the *adamah*" the first human, who was known accordingly as "Adam." Here the Flood was described as covering the "ground," the same material that in God's hands had become Adam—clearly a local and much more limited reality than "planet Earth." Since this was the narrator's second indication of the territory that the Flood would cover, it seems almost certain that in the earlier instance the narrator was thinking of a Flood over an area of "land" rather than the entire planet Earth. The ancient Hebrew words *adamah* ("ground") and *'erets* ("land") were clearly related, with *adamah* closer to "soil" and *'erets* closer to "territory" (as in "the land of Egypt"), whereas the modern concepts of "ground" and "planet Earth" are fundamentally, even radically, dissimilar.

Genesis 7:3, 4 is not the only time that parallel concepts enunciated in close proximity help Ian Michael to get back into the Genesis narrator's mind and thus acquire a better understanding of what he was thinking. A few verses later the narrator reported that "all flesh died that moved on the land [*'erets*]," that "every living thing on dry land [*adamah*] . . . died," and that "every living thing on the face of the ground [*adamah*]" was "blotted out" (vv. 21–23, OHV). As before, here are three references to the extent of the Flood's devastation. Two of them are clearly limited to land-like entities. It seems highly unlikely that the third reference to the extent of the Flood should be rendered in English as "earth" and taken to mean that the Great Flood was global in extent. But that is what Ian Michael is almost certain to do when Hebrew-to-English translations render *'erets* as "earth" rather than "land."

Gen. 7:11. In the six-hundredth year of Noah's life, in the second month, on the seventeenth day of the month—on that day all the **torrential outpourings** of the **primeval waters** burst forth, and the **flood gates** of the **sky** were opened (OHV).

Gen. 7:11. In the six-hundredth year of Noah's life, in the second month, on the seventeenth day of the month, on that day all the **fountains of the great deep** burst forth, and **the windows of the heavens** were opened (NRSV).

THE GREAT FLOOD: HUGE QUANTITIES OF WATER OVERWHELMING CONTINENTS, OR SOMETHING ELSE?

Figuring out how Moshe heard or read the Flood narrative and understood that unprecedented catastrophe is a major challenge for Ian Michael. Unless he is a most unusual student of the Bible, he is going to read the Flood accounts not as the theology they actually are but as scientific (or proto-scientific or pseudo-scientific) accounts of an event in which huge quantities of water, held onto the surface of the planet by gravity, overwhelmed and reshaped the continents. He is intellectually curious and college educated, and this is the way the accounts have been read by most educated Christians ever since the natural laws that apply to very large amounts of water were formulated.

Moshe, on the other hand, understood the Flood entirely as an act of God, who, distressed by human wickedness, let the primeval waters (*tehom*) loose from the bounds that had been established by the *raqia'*/vault at Creation. For Moshe it was God's act from beginning to end. Initially, God determined to wipe out all humanity, destroying it along with the land on which it lived. But on reading this, Ian Michael is puzzled and frustrated. He needs (and expects) a hydrologically sound description of where the water came from—perhaps subterranean aquifers, or a water-containing, earth-surrounding shell, or a passing water-rich comet. The water that overwhelmed the whole of planet Earth must have come from somewhere.

Unfortunately, the "somewheres" described in the Bible account are not of much help. To put it bluntly, the sources of the Flood waters described in Genesis are not scientifically credible. Ian Michael knows that there is now no *raqia'* between himself and deep space, and certainly no ocean held in place above the *raqia'*, and he has never heard of any scientific evidence that there were ever such strange entities in the past. So he is puzzled. What he reads in Genesis 6–8 seems to be an account of a catastrophic natural event, but the description he reads lacks the scientific credibility that he expects will characterize a divinely inspired account of an unimaginable *natural* catastrophe.

Gen. 7:19–21. **The water swelled** so much on the **land** that all the high mountains under the whole **sky** were covered. . . . And all flesh died that moved on the land—birds, farm animals, wild animals, . . . and all human beings (OHV).

Gen. 7:19–21. **The waters swelled** so mightily on the **earth** that all the high mountains under the whole **heaven** were covered. . . . And all flesh died that moved on the earth, birds, domestic animals, wild animals . . . , and all human beings (NRSV).

"WATERS SWELLING MIGHTILY" SOUNDS LIKE A HYDROLOGICAL CATASTROPHE IN THE REALM OF NATURE

If Ian Michael reads the Flood narrative starting after God's pronouncement, "I have determined to make an end of all flesh" and skips "He blotted out everything alive on the face of the ground—human beings and animals," he might very well conclude that the Flood was indeed a natural catastrophe occasioned by a vast excess of water over all of Earth. But the Biblical record shows that it was not that at all. It was God's Flood from beginning to end. At that time and place, there were no such things as "natural catastrophes," for there was no "realm of nature" in which a catastrophe could occur. Everything that happened or could happen was the result of humans acting or God acting. The Great Flood was a catastrophe of such magnitude that only God could have caused it.

IN "A FLOOD OF BIBLICAL PROPORTIONS," WHERE DID THE WATER COME FROM AND WHERE DID IT GO?

Moshe heard of a God who remembered Noah and the animals that were with him in the ark (Gen. 8:1). That same God confined the *tehom* once more by closing the subterranean channels through which the primeval waters had reached the surface and resealed the channels overhead through which the primeval waters had inundated the land.

Then, the narrative continues, after attending to these critical matters, God ended the Flood by sending a great wind to dry up the waters. Ian Michael is now doubly frustrated. He does not recognize *tehom* as a scientifically credible source of "a Flood of Biblical proportions," so he still has no workable understanding of where all the water came from since he does not believe that there is a *raqia'*, or vault, above his head with unlimited water storage behind and above it. And he does not know where the water went; he is quite certain that although a great wind might move the floodwater around a bit, it is certainly not going to dry it up because he knows that water evaporated by wind will sooner or later precipitate as rain. All of this frustration comes from Ian Michael's attempt to read an ancient two-explanacept theological narrative with his modern three-explanacept scientific mind. The project just doesn't—and cannot—succeed.

A much more challenging problem that Ian Michael may not have even noticed is still ahead. No single text neatly encapsulates it, but if he reads carefully, he discovers that the sun moved around Moshe's world. Ian Michael knows for a fact that exactly the opposite is true: Earth is what moves, revolving around the sun and rotating on its own axis. These two mental constructions of reality are as dissimilar as it is possible to be. Geocentrism (Moshe's reality) and heliocentrism (Ian Michael's reality) are 180 degrees apart. The Genesis narrative confirms geocentrism for Moshe. It still, in the twenty-first century, confirms geocentrism for Ian Michael, though he is unlikely to read it that way. It is to this discrepancy that we turn next.

Chapter Nine

A TALE OF TWO COSMOLOGIES

Geocentric versus Heliocentric

Upon hearing the familiar words, "In the beginning God created the heavens and the earth" (Gen. 1:1, NKJV, NIV), Ian Michael inevitably pictures some sort of heliocentric cosmology, with a centrally placed sun in a "solar system" and with everything else circling it. It might be a collection of planets—some gigantic and gaseous, some comparatively small and rocky—in orbit. Or perhaps a single planet comes into his mind's eye, a planet shrouded in darkness and covered with water. Depending upon how many astronomy books he has read or how many TV shows on cosmology he has seen, Ian Michael's imagination might produce a globe that is cold and dark, with North and South America on its surface, orbiting the sun. Whatever the mental image, it will almost certainly be heliocentric, having the sun at the center; for anyone living in the twenty-first century it is virtually impossible to imagine anything else in three dimensions.

On the other hand, when Moshe heard or read the corresponding sentences in Hebrew three millennia or more ago, he did not envision anything like Ian Michael's mental images. We are certain of this because, for one thing, it was quite impossible for him to imagine his *'erets* ("land") as a planet; he (like all other human beings) was completely unaware that such an entity existed anywhere. For another thing, it was obvious to him that the ground beneath his feet was stationary; it was the "greater light" in the sky (Gen. 1:16) that moved, not the land on which he lived.

Many references in Moshe's sacred scrolls affirmed his understanding of reality. He took geocentrism for granted in the Genesis 1 account of Creation week: the sky (*shemayim*) and the land (*'erets*) were brought into existence by God, who proceeded to create vegetation (Day Three), as well as the "greater" and "lesser" lights and the stars (Day Four). The "greater" light was intended to "give light upon the land" that already existed; it was "set" in the "dome" that had been created to protect that land from the primeval *tehom*. The "greater" light was also to mark the passage of time—it was not created to serve as the gravitational center of a group of rotating spheres. The function of the land as the stable basis of human and animal life was affirmed poetically in other passages of the Hebrew canon: "The pillars of the earth are the LORD's, and on them he has set the world" (1 Sam. 2:8b), "The world is firmly established, it shall never be moved" (1 Chron. 16:30b). "The LORD . . . has established the world;

it shall never be moved" (Ps 93:1). "You set the earth on its foundations, so that it shall never be shaken" (Ps. 104:5).

The main support for Moshe's geocentric worldview came from the simple fact that it was obvious; all he needed to do was to look around him, below and above. His understanding of how the land and the "greater light" were related was based upon what he saw every day: the land was stationary, and the "greater light" moved across the sky. Indeed, the "greater light" moved from east to west across the sky above his land once each day—and under it each night. Given that his only source of information about the interrelationships of the land and the "greater light" was his naked-eye astronomy, unenhanced by any telescopic observations, no other understanding was possible. Physical reality was totally geocentric: the land was at the center of everything; the "greater light" and the stars (like the moon) moved around it.

In this worldview Moshe was, of course, neither unique nor original. It was the only possible worldview from long before his own time until long after. In fact, it was the only worldview up to the sixteenth century. Martin Luther understood created reality in this geocentric fashion as late as 1534, when he published his copiously illustrated German Bible. The workshop of Lucas Cranach had produced page after page of artwork, and one of the most spectacular examples showed God at the top of a colorful picture of a lavish earth.[1] At the center of the earth-scene, Adam and Eve benignly ruled over the animals around them. Near the bottom, in a large body of water, was leviathan with a crocodilian snout and a massive reptilian tail. A firmament with an embedded sun,

1. Stephan Füssel and Benedikt Taschen, *The Bible in Pictures: Illustrations from the Workshop of Lucas Cranach* (1534) (Cologne, Germany: Taschen, 2009).

moon, and stars rotated around the earth, and farther out, a shell of water was kept in place by the interposed firmament. This spherical earth-at-the-center, stationary, with everything else in motion around it, had been the standard worldview from at least the time of the Greeks and Romans.

But change was imminent. In 1543, just nine years after Luther's German Bible appeared, the mathematician and astronomer Nicolaus Copernicus published *De revolutionibus orbium coelestium* (*On the Revolutions of the Heavenly Spheres*) shortly before his death. (According to legend, he first saw the final printed pages of the book on the day he died.) Luther had heard about Copernicus's new ideas and didn't accept any of them; he thought Copernicus was spouting nonsense. Not one to mince his words, Luther called Copernicus both a fool and an astrologer,[2] although he knew full well that Copernicus prided himself on his competence in astronomy. In 1533 the received wisdom was the same as it had been for thousands of years, and Luther's fellow Reformer Philipp Melanchthon agreed. "The eyes are witness that the heavens revolve in the space of twenty-four hours," Melanchthon said. "But certain men . . . have concluded that the earth moves. . . . Now it is a want of honesty and decency to assert such notions publicly, and the example is pernicious."[3] So from long before the time of Moshe He'eb to the time of Martin Luther, everybody everywhere could envision only a geocentric arrangement of earth, sun, and stars. No other mental

2. "People give ear to an upstart astrologer who strove to show that the earth revolves, not the heaven or the firmament, the sun and the moon. . . . This fool wishes to reverse the entire science of astronomy; but Sacred Scripture tells us that Josue [Joshua] commanded the sun to stand still, and not the earth." Jerome J. Langford, *Galileo, Science and the Church*, 3rd ed. (Ann Arbor, MI: University of Michigan Press, 1992), 35.

3. Philipp Melanchthon, *Initia doctrinae physicae*, *Corpus Reformatorum*, 13:216, 217.

image was available with which to understand and to mentally picture the Biblical assertion that "in the beginning God created the heavens and the earth."

But for the past four hundred years the opposite has been the case. Ever since that "fool" and "astrologer" who was "lacking in honesty and decency" saw things differently, no one who has heard of Copernicus—to say nothing of Johannes Kepler and Galileo Galilei—has envisioned a cosmos with Earth at the center. For Ian Michael such a view is utterly impossible because he has seen photographic images of planet Earth suspended in space rising over the moon. He has seen pictures from the Hubble telescope; he has read newspaper accounts of asteroid strikes in remote Russian cities. He knows that the earth is tiny compared to the sun and exerts only a minuscule fraction of the sun's gravitational attraction. Furthermore, he knows that the solar system to which Earth belongs is a small part of the Milky Way, which in turn is a minor part of the known universe. In the light of all this information, Ian Michael cannot escape (much less deny) his awareness that, despite what his eyes tell him, it is the earth that moves, and it moves around the sun. In short, physical reality is heliocentric. Given all this cosmological information, it is impossible for Ian Michael to suppose that the sun revolves around Earth—just as it was impossible for Moshe to suppose that the land on which he lived revolved around the "greater light."

Although this is a relatively recent situation, Ian Michael's heliocentric view has been a significant part of human understanding during almost the entire time that the Hebrew Bible has been available in an English translation (beginning with William Tyndale's version of the Pentateuch in 1530). Ian Michael's mental constructs are therefore essentially identical to those of the scholars who have produced the Bible translations upon which he depends. That Ian Michael and Bible translators have, for nearly five hundred years, had similar heliocentric cosmologies is significant.

HELIOCENTRISM REPLACES GEOCENTRISM

Luther and Melanchthon were thoroughgoing geocentrists, as Moshe had been two and a half millennia earlier. True, in the intervening centuries it became evident to those who were interested in such matters that Earth was not flat and supported by pillars but was instead a sphere in space; and the Greek philosopher Eratosthenes (276–194 BCE) had calculated its diameter with remarkable accuracy. But neither Eratosthenes nor anyone else before the sixteenth century had any doubts that the sphere of Earth was fixed at the center of cosmic reality. Like Moshe, they were geocentrists through and through. By the time of Luther and Melanchthon, the earth-sphere was pictured as the center of many spherical shells, the closest shell being identified as the Biblical "firmament" of Genesis 1.[4]

Two events were largely responsible for transforming geocentric into heliocentric cosmology. The first, already mentioned, was the publication of Copernicus's *On the Revolutions of the Heavenly Spheres* in 1543. The second, seventy-two years later, was an investigation by the Roman Inquisition in 1615, of the Copernican theory. That investigation led to Cardinal Bellarmine admonishing Galileo "not to hold, teach, or defend the Copernican theory in any way whatever, either orally or in writing." Although Galileo was found guilty (at trial in 1633) and placed under house arrest until his death (though not imprisoned, much less

4. Füssel and Taschen, *The Bible in Pictures*.

tortured),[5] history has judged both that Copernicus and Galileo were right and that the era's leading theologians (Protestant as well as Catholic) were wrong.

But how and why were they wrong? Therein lies a problem. Although for four hundred years it has been generally agreed that Galileo was right in that our physical reality is indeed heliocentric, were not the Catholic theologians advising the Inquisition correct in their reading of the Bible?

HOW IAN MICHAEL'S GENESIS BECAME SO DIFFERENT FROM MOSHE'S

The difference between a sun-centered cosmology and an earth-centered one is profound. One wonders how it is possible that the same Hebrew text that so clearly confirmed Moshe's geocentric cosmology is now almost always read by Ian Michael as a description of heliocentric cosmology. Here is our explanation of why events unfolded in this unforeseen fashion.

Observing Moshe in the preceding chapters, we have followed his narrative path as he read or heard an original hearers' version of Genesis 1–11. At the same time we have also followed the very different narrative path of Ian Michael as he now reads the same Bible chapters but in NRSV, NIV, NKJV, or some other recent English version. In the process, it has become evident that Ian Michael's narrative diverges diametrically from Moshe's. The difference is already apparent by the end of the first sentence (Gen. 1:1); and by the end of the first Creation narrative (Gen. 2:4a), Ian Michael finds himself in almost a "parallel universe." It is here that the monumental disconnect between religion and science has arisen and persisted.[6]

---

5. See Ronald L. Numbers, ed., *Galileo Goes to Jail And Other Myths about Science and Religion* (Cambridge, MA: Harvard University Press, 2001), 68–78.

6. This so-called disconnect is taken up again in the afterword.

For Moshe, things were very different. Despite the strangeness (to us) of the world he inhabited, the narratives of Genesis 1–11 involved no chasm between his religion and his common sense. He recognized that what he heard (or read) was all *theology*—about God and Moshe's relation to God. He found no science (or proto-science) in the narrative and, hence, no scientific findings with which he had to wrestle. For Moshe, Genesis was *all* theology—it was "words about God's Being, God's actions, God's desires (for us)."[7] Since it is, in part, words about God's actions—what *God does*—he experiences no disconnect at all. His world may be strange indeed to Ian Michael, but it is completely coherent to Moshe. God can do anything that is inherently doable (excluding only things like making a square circle or making an event not to have happened), particularly if he is doing it for the benefit of humans—of whom Moshe is representative and the one to whom Genesis is addressed.

This raises several obvious questions: (1) Why is retro-translation necessary to recapture Moshe's world? Why do not the carefully produced English translations that Ian Michael reads accomplish the same purpose? (2) If the distressing disconnect between science and religion is no more complicated than the difference between the way Moshe read or heard Genesis 1–11 *then* and the way Ian Michael reads it *now*, how did this marked difference between the two readings of Genesis come about? (3) Why have translators not rendered *'erets* as "land" in Genesis 1–11 as they have done in the rest of Genesis and the rest of the Hebrew Bible?

---

7. See Bull and Guy, *God, Land, and the Great Flood*, 190. "The purpose of Scripture is to give insight into the meaning of our existence by revealing who God is, what God does, and what God wants for us."

THE PERSISTENT DISCONNECT THAT BEGAN WITH GALILEO

The world of Moshe was utterly geocentric. No ancient Hebrew doubted that all heavenly bodies revolved around the *'erets* or that the *'erets* had been placed at the center of everything by God. Indeed, God had created it for that purpose, to occupy that very position. Its stability, its fixedness, was convincing evidence of God's plan and power (Ps. 104:5). Galileo, however, insisted otherwise. He claimed that the earth did move and that the sun was stationary. Furthermore, he insisted that the earth *moved around the sun* rather than the sun moving around the earth. Even more disturbing, with his newly improved telescope, Galileo saw that some heavenly bodies (such as moons) revolved around heavenly bodies other than Earth, proving that Earth was *not* the center of everything. These radical notions understandably upset the religious authorities of the time, going against the clear word of Scripture. They also violated common sense. One did not have to be a religious authority to see that the sun moved across the sky and that Earth did not move at all (except in earthquakes, and then not very far).

Eventually, as we all know, Galileo was proved right, and the religious authorities *along with the Genesis text* were proved wrong, at least on the matter of whether the sun revolved around Earth or Earth revolved around the sun. That the Genesis text was incorrect on this matter came to be accepted both by religious authorities and by Bible readers everywhere. Or did it?

A case can be made that the controversy initiated by Galileo peering through his telescope has not yet, to this very day, been finally settled. Yes, scientists and laypersons alike have agreed that the earth does revolve around the sun; but many scholars insist that the Biblical claims come to us from a primitive society that did not have access to anything more than "visual astronomy." As a consequence, the Bible could do no other than report what was obvious when the only available evidence was what could be seen by the unaided eye. Besides, since we still regularly talk about "sunrise" and "sunset," why should we expect anything more from the ancient Hebrews?

Thus some, or perhaps most, Bible readers since Galileo's time put to rest the "Galileo controversy" without ever really conceding that Moshe's conviction (that the sun went around his *'erets*) was *incorrect*. They cut Moshe some slack because it looked to him as if it were the sun that moved. True enough, but they should rather have cut him some slack because his insistence that the sun moved was not an "observation" in the realm of science at all. The "greater light" was *God's creation*, and it did what it did at God's command; end of discussion. Calling it "proto-science" and thus letting Moshe off the hook has done no one a favor. It wasn't proto-science—a happening in the natural realm—it was *theology*. It was a description of God's action for Moshe's benefit. Failing to make that critical distinction meant that the problem was not solved but just "kicked down the road" and that it would come back again in the form of Ian Michael's Bible-reading dilemma. Is the Bible to be read literally, or is it to be read figuratively?

After the fuss and kerfuffle precipitated by Copernicus and Galileo died down, Bible translators, along with most readers, returned to the text, hoping and often fully expecting that "divine inspiration" would guarantee that the Bible, if properly translated, would confirm the most up-to-date scientific cosmology. They seem to have expected, consciously or unconsciously, that the Bible presaged advances in science and was waiting for cosmology and astrophysics to catch up.

That, however, has not happened. Genesis 1–11, no matter how or by whom it has been translated, has not outlined scientific truth ahead of major discoveries. Ian Michael's reading of Genesis, though different from Moshe's, has not turned out to be a CliffsNotes version of modern astronomy. There still exists a huge disconnect between science as commonly understood and Genesis as Ian Michael usually reads it. And, as time passes and new translations appear, the disconnect only gets wider and deeper.

THE EXPLANACEPT OF "NATURE" ARRIVES

One of the reasons for this increasing chasm comes from the development of other intellectual capabilities that were just beginning to appear during Galileo's era. In the late sixteenth and early seventeenth centuries, science as a discipline was just emerging. The habits of thought that led Galileo to reach and disseminate his startling conclusions were being shared by others, and the idea was dawning also on other minds that regularities existed in nature that, if understood and codified, might enhance human mastery of nature. In time these regularities were dignified as the "laws of nature," and the methods and processes that led to their discovery came to be known as science.

Early astronomers did not question that discoveries made using the procedures of science were correctly categorized as discoveries in the realm of "nature." For the first time in human history a new explanatory concept—in our jargon, a new explanacept—appeared. No longer were there only two explanacepts—divine action and human action—to account for everything that existed or happened. With the arrival of "nature," a third explanatory concept existed, and Genesis 1–11, previously read from start to finish as *theology*, now began to be read in part as theology and in part as a description of nature (science). For the first time, it was interpreted as "words about divine activity" intertwined with "words about natural occurrences." As such it seemed obvious to the newly minted scientists that the task ahead was, first of all, to separate Genesis into its two newly defined components. Though a reasonable assumption, it was a fraught one. Reading Genesis in that manner made it inevitable that theological statements, originally written as descriptions of God's action, would now, 2,500 years after they were first written, be reinterpreted as statements about nature and, therefore, science (or proto-science). Once that happened, they were subjected to the same vetting procedures that were applied to scientific claims generally.

If the Genesis narratives of Creation had been left as theological statements about what God was understood (by Moshe) to have done, the disconnect between religion and science might never have materialized. Ian Michael's Genesis could have been understood as describing (as Moshe's Genesis did) how God had dealt creatively with the preexisting water and darkness by speaking light into existence and creating a *raqia'* to corral the *tehom*, ensuring that the *'erets* would support Moshe's existence. Reading the ancient Hebrew in this way, Ian Michael would have understood that the Creation story was a story about God's delight in and care for humanity. That it was about the pleasure God experienced in creating and protecting humanity, and seeing to it that the sky, the land, the plants, and the animals in all their mind-boggling richness would be there for Moshe and his descendants to enjoy. Ian Michael's Genesis would not have become an invitation to controversy, a book to fight over, a series of hidden meanings to be deciphered. It would continue to be what it had always been—a tangible expression of God-in-action for the benefit of human beings.

BIBLE TRANSLATIONS AS REFLECTIONS OF THEIR TIMES

In the English-speaking world of the early seventeenth century, the time of Galileo's conflict with religious authorities was precisely the time when translators were working on improved versions of the Bible. In 1611 the venerable King James Version appeared. The translators, largely selected from the faculties of Oxford and Cambridge, though not scientists themselves, were, like all intellectuals of the time, immersed in the exciting physics, mathematics, and astronomy of the nascent scientific disciplines. Only four years after the publication of the KJV, Copernicus's writings and Galileo's laudatory accompanying letter were submitted to the Inquisition.

The KJV translators could not have realized that the newly conceptualized realm of "nature" and its investigation as "science" would radically change the general understanding of Genesis 1–11 and affect the rest of the Bible as well. This was not because the translators had any difficulty accepting the notion of "nature" itself—after all, the material world was very much a part of God's creation, and it operated consistently under "laws" that were as much an expression of God's will as were the Ten Commandments. Everything that happened in nature was simply God's action, one step removed.

What the readers as well as the translators appear not to have recognized while they were becoming conversant with the newly conceived realm of nature was that it was a realm of which Moshe knew nothing. At the time the translators were working on the KJV, they seem to have forgotten that "nature" was a realm that had come into human consciousness only recently; in fact, it had emerged largely after Tyndale first translated the Hebrew Bible directly into English in 1530. Tyndale had paid for his enterprise and diligence with his life, having been executed as a heretic in 1536. Only seventy-five years later, the KJV translators were honored by King James for their scholarship. During this period, nature, both as a reality and as an explanation, came to be recognized, and during the same time, science came to be recognized as an intellectual discipline.

Although Moshe could have known nothing of such developments, Ian Michael knows them so well that he cannot imagine a world in which "nature," "natural laws," and "science" are not readily understood by all who have had even a modest awareness of reality. Ever since 1611, Bible translators, too, have taken for granted the "natural world" and "natural regularities." Consequently, they have (largely unconsciously) translated Genesis to conform as much as possible to the growing understanding of nature's "laws," the recognized regularities that characterize material reality.

Moshe, of course, would have been nonplussed by the transformation of his theological narrative. "To begin with" (Gen. 1:1, OHV; Hebrew *bereshith*) has been consistently elevated to "In the beginning," which in Ian Michael's mind often refers to the coming into being of planet Earth, if not the solar system or even the entire universe. Moshe's mundane "sky" has been transformed into "heavens," which almost immediately morph astronomically into "starry heavens"; and Moshe's beloved "land"—really his *homeland*—becomes Ian Michael's planet Earth. Once the very first *'erets* in Genesis 1:1 became "earth" (as it has been consistently translated from Tyndale on), the subsequent pattern for Genesis 1–11 was established.

Thus Moshe's comparatively simple yet profound theological narrative has become a problematic cosmological description of planets and stars, of space and time, and especially of the earth as Earth, the planet we call home. As a result, Moshe's straightforward-for-the-time *theological* narrative has become the underlying, and totally unnecessary, hermeneutical cause of the spiritually and theologically disastrous disconnect between religion and science.

So what exactly is this Bible, this volume that has been translated into English from its original Hebrew and is now proving so perplexing to Ian Michael?

Chapter Ten

NOT A "BOOK" OR A "LIBRARY" BUT A "CURATED COLLECTION"

Who Cares?

Of course, the Bible is a *book*; in fact, it is *the* Book. That's what the word *Bible* literally means, coming from the Latin *biblia* and recognizable in English words like "bibliography" and "bibliophile." And the reasons for calling the Bible a "book" are obvious. It looks like a book, it is bound as a book, and except in very rare instances, usually for scholarly purposes, the contents are printed and sold together as a single item. If queried, most Bible readers (even those who write books for a living) consider it a book and have thought of it that way for their entire lives. Without further information as to what is at stake, Ian Michael, our quintessential modern Christian, considers the question Is the Bible really a book?

rather odd—at a minimum. He may even think that raising the question borders on sacrilege or, more likely, simple foolishness.

But if Ian Michael is reminded that the Hebrew Bible was produced by many different writers (probably more than forty and possibly even more)—and that it was written over half a millennium or longer, the question, though still odd, begins to make sense. True enough, multiple authors can and often do contribute to a single book, but such situations usually involve one or more editors to select and harmonize the contributions of the various authors and ensure that the various contributions constitute a coherent whole. But no such editorial process is identified by extra-Biblical sources, much less by anything in the Bible itself.[1]

If Ian Michael also learns that some of the Hebrew Bible writers lived hundreds of miles away from the hill country of Palestine in places like the capital cities of Babylon or Persia, what then? And to complicate matters still further, it is likely that some of the writings were originally composed in languages other than Hebrew. With this additional information, will Ian Michael, reading his English translation, still regard the Bible as a *book*? Our guess is that with this added knowledge, Ian Michael will probably agree that the Bible is more like a library than like a typical book, and most of all it is like a curated collection of materials, a kind of sacred archive. And if, because it is bound as a book and sold as a book, it has to be categorized as a book, it is certainly a highly unusual book.

The answer to this apparently simple question, What is the Bible? is important because a modern interpreter of the Bible (and we all interpret the Biblical text every time we read it in any

1. The familiar assertion in 2 Peter 1:21 that "holy men of God spoke as they were moved by the Holy Spirit" (NKJV) refers to the initiation of the divine message, not its evaluation or preservation.

language) travels down one of many different interpretive paths, depending on the perhaps unconscious answer to the question What is the Bible? One interpretation results if Ian Michael thinks he is reading part of an extended document by a single Author (the Holy Spirit), for whom the various human writers functioned as amanuenses or secretaries. Another, quite different interpretation results if Ian Michael believes he is reading a series of essays produced by various *contributors* and harmonized by the Holy Spirit as Editor-in-Chief. If the Bible is thus understood as a sort of anthology, then change and increasing clarity will seem likely as the various contributors wrestled with the transcendental topic of God and grew in their understanding of it. As Moshe and his descendants told and retold the ancient narratives, under the Holy Spirit's guidance they came to understand God's being, intentions, and actions ever more clearly.

A third—and, we believe, preferable—interpretation results if Ian Michael believes he is reading an item in a curated collection of diverse contributions on various matters from many different authors addressing different issues in different places and different times, but all concerned with the same broad theological topic—who God is, what God does, and what God wants for all of us. If this third view of the Bible is correct, and we are convinced that it is, the Bible as a whole may well reflect increasing clarity, depth, and breadth of understanding as the centuries passed as well as differing perspectives depending on cultural contexts and personal circumstances. This centuries-long process, overseen and guided by the Holy Spirit, produced a curated collection—the Bible—that Ian Michael can read all at once in the twenty-first century.

So we raise a number of questions: What is the Hebrew canon, more commonly known as the *Hebrew Bible*? What best describes the approximately five-hundred-year-long process that produced it? Did the individual writers, separated by hundreds of years of history and culture, have similar (even if not identical) understandings of God and God's actions? Is there evidence of intervention by the Holy Spirit to correct misunderstandings of what God was doing in the world? Have factual errors in history or misconceptions of the way the world works been corrected—geocentrism updated by the Holy Spirit to heliocentrism, for example? Or were the various Hebrew authors firmly fixed in the understandings of their times and cultures? Is the understanding of God and what God did and did not do in the world consistent from Genesis to Malachi, or does it reflect increasing clarity in the matter?

GOD OF THE HEBREW CANON, GOD OF THE NEW TESTAMENT

Even more important (as best we can determine from the texts that they have left us), did authors grow in understanding of who God was, what God did, and what God wanted for them? In other words, was the God of the Hebrew Bible identical to the God of the New Testament? The answer to this last question is, of course, no—as Jesus Himself confirmed. Jesus spent much of His ministry correcting the misunderstandings held by His Jewish contemporaries—misunderstandings based on what they understood the Hebrew canon to have said about God. For example, six times in the Sermon on the Mount as reported by Matthew, Jesus began a corrective comment with the phrase, "You have heard that it was said" followed by, "But I say to you" (Matt. 5:21, 27, 31, 33, 38, 43).

The changes that Jesus proposed were substantive; some went to the heart of traditional Hebrew theology and ethics. He obviously viewed the Hebrew canon as eminently correctable. Indeed, He clearly viewed the Hebrew Bible as greatly in need of correction, particularly in matters related to the anticipated Messiah and the role that the Messiah would play in the future of the nation. He gave no indication that the Holy Spirit had functioned as Editor-in-Chief of the sacred scrolls and melded the contributions of the early Hebrew writers into an integrated and consistent whole, uniform in its understanding of God from the Law (*Torah*) through the Prophets (*Nebi'im*) to the [Sacred] Writings (*Kethubim*).

If the Hebrew canon is indeed a curated collection of contributions from many different writers who lived in communities that were separated widely in both space and time, we in the twenty-first century want to know what may be the implications for us in our reading of the sacred text. As Christians we are confident that the Holy Spirit played an essential role in the motivation and origination of the ancient Hebrew documents, but we wonder just what that role was if it was not that of Editor-in-Chief and Guarantor of error-free history, theology, and proto-science. In particular, we want to know whether each writer had an accurate (perhaps inerrant?) understanding of God. Pursuing the matter further, we would like to know what role the Holy Spirit played if not ensuring that this was the case. These are important questions. The answers affect our understanding of the Bible—whether we think of it as a unified book, trans-generational library, or curated collection. We want to know as specifically as we can what the task is that Scripture has performed so successfully that it has survived and thrived for thousands of years.

Whatever its mission, the Hebrew canon accomplishes it largely by recounting narratives. There are narratives of Adam and Eve, Cain and Abel, Noah and the Great Flood, Nimrod and the Tower of Babel—all telling us more about how God was understood and experienced by the tellers than about the particular characters in the narratives. So we wonder how the particular narratives were selected for that honor, why they were deemed valuable enough to be copied and thus preserved for posterity. At a time when copying a written document was extremely laborious, it was not unusual for persons to dedicate their lives to this task; and we would like to know why they did it, for had they not done it, there would be no Hebrew canon—and perhaps no New Testament either. And we wonder about the differences between Moshe's directly copied (and untranslated) texts and Ian Michael's various English versions translated at various times from copies of copies of copies of the original Hebrew texts.

CHANGES IN "GOD KNOWLEDGE" OVER TIME AS ILLUSTRATED BY BIBLICAL NARRATIVES

Whether we regard the Bible as a book, a library, or a curated collection, it is clear that the major purpose of Scripture is to help readers at all times and in all places to understand what God intends for humans created in God's image. So if we ask whether the writer(s) of Genesis[2] give us time-transcendent answers to these three implied questions, the best (although perhaps surprising) answer is, No, they don't."

Actually, for much of Genesis, these important questions are not answered directly at all. At first glance, we see a series of stories about people and their relationships—Adam and Eve, Cain and Abel, Noah and his family, Abraham and Lot,

---

2. Although there is no direct internal or external assertion of multiple authors of Genesis, the variety of literary styles, vocabulary, and theological concerns indicate convincingly that the text we have is the work of more than one mind. Hence our practice of referring to "the writer(s)" or "the author(s)" of Genesis.

Sarah and Hagar, Isaac and Rebekah, Jacob and Esau, Leah and Rachel—and we are not yet halfway through Genesis. Many of the stories do mention God from time to time, but often it seems only as one more-or-less important element in the story. Of course, we can deduce from the stories something about how the characters viewed God; but we can do this only by "reading between the lines," and it is clear that these views changed over time. The "God-pictures" provided by the authors of the Hebrew Bible changed with the passing years as the Israelites experienced slavery, escape, nationhood, military dominance, monarchy, and wars with the regional superpowers of Assyria, Babylon, and Egypt. As these God-pictures changed, improved, and faded over time, we recognize the Hebrew canon not only as a sacred library but also as a curated collection of stories about and understandings of God—a theological saga.

The Hebrew canon is a written record of what God wanted for His people at various times in their history. According to Moses, for example, YHWH wanted a fence built around the base of the mountain of law-giving lest the people come too close and die (Exod. 19:12). But later, according to Jesus, God expected the descendants of those people to come fearlessly into the divine presence with the assurance that God, their Father, would supply food, drink, and clothing to His children (Luke 12:30).

Regarding what God does, the changes over time were particularly striking. YHWH brought the rain[3] and laid up in His storehouse the treasures of ice and snow (Job 37:6; 38:22), determined whether women bore children (or not), and the list goes on. "What God does" has changed so remarkably that in the twenty-first century Ian Michael does not view God as *directly* responsible for the weather, pregnancy, or much of anything else.

3. Gen. 2:5; Exod. 9:33; Lev. 26:4, 1 Sam. 12:17, 18.

And then there is the nature and character of God: "who God is." Though ontologically and ethically God does not change, the Bible writers' understanding of "what God does" and "what God wants for us" certainly changed; and as these aspects of God-knowledge changed, the understanding of "who God is" necessarily changed as well. Moreover, if Moshe, lacking the explanatory concept of *nature*, conflated thinking and talking about natural regularities with thinking and talking about God, with the result that both kinds of thinking and talking were *theology*, then his understanding of "what God does" was inevitably very different from Ian Michael's.

In general the writers of the collection of materials that became the Hebrew canon communicated their understanding of God by telling stories, usually about their forebears. Before these stories were written, the patriarchs of Moshe's tribe repeated them orally, handing them down for generations. Rather than giving us a list of truths about the Divine accompanied by supporting evidence and arguments, they chose this form of communication because this was how they had come to their understanding of God. In the process of telling, retelling, and eventually writing down their founding narratives[4] and prophetic insights, the ancient Hebrews produced Holy Scripture for themselves and for us.

The result is a "book" in the sense that it is a collection of stories and messages that are regularly packaged together. It is

---

4. See C. S. Lewis, *Reflections on the Psalms* (New York: Harcourt, Brace, 1958), 110, 111: "Stories do not reproduce their species like mice. They are told by men. Each re-teller either repeats exactly what his predecessor had told him or else changes it. . . . When a series of such re-tellings turns a creation story which at first had almost no religious or metaphysical meaning into a story which achieves the idea of true Creation and of a transcendent Creator (as *Genesis* does), then nothing will make me believe that some of the re-tellers, or some one of them, has not been guided by God."

a "library" in the sense that it contains the writings of a wide range of authors and a range of literary forms and theological ideas. And it is a "curated collection" in the sense that it is the integrated product of deliberate effort over a long period. It is also "revelation" because its narratives and messages document a progressive understanding of God achieved over centuries by a nation of farmers, herdsmen, political leaders, and visionaries.

WHAT ALL THIS SAYS ABOUT THE NATURE OF SCRIPTURE

In noting the divergent narrative paths that Moshe originally traversed and that Ian Michael now follows, several conclusions become apparent. First, not only was Moshe's ancient world very different from Ian Michael's present world, but much of the difference involves the realm of nature. Forces, objects, and regularities are present in Ian Michael's world that were not imagined (or even imaginable) in Moshe's world. Similarly, realities and forces were recognized in Moshe's world that are incomprehensible in Ian Michael's world (and which, he is pretty sure, did not actually exist in Moshe's world either), such as the *raqia'* and the *tehom*. Puzzles like these arise from a careful reading of the Hebrew text of Genesis; and, depending upon the English version Ian Michael reads, they may or may not be obvious to him. Whether he recognizes them depends to a great extent on the words that the translator(s) of a particular version deemed "right and proper."

This state of affairs can be unsettling, to say the least. The Bible is the Word of God whether it is regarded as a book, a library, or a curated collection. Ideally, Ian Michael's understanding of the Hebrew canon should not be at the mercy of what particular translators may have deemed "right and proper" to convey the author's meaning to English readers. Furthermore, it might (ironically) appear that our recommended process of retro-translation actually worsens matters because the retro-translated text of Genesis 1–11 depicts Moshe's world as a very strange place indeed. Ian Michael finds it mind-boggling, for example, to seriously attempt to envision a sky-vault above his head, confining and thus controlling the *tehom*. He has grown up with a day that is exactly twenty-four hours long—from one midnight to the next—and finds it mentally unsettling to enter a conceptual world in which a day consists of twelve hours but of variable length,[5] depending on the time of year. In Moshe's world, "night" was in a completely different category from "day," with no "hours" at all because no sun was visible by which he could tell time. The list of conceptual differences goes on and on, and with each additional dissimilarity, the fundamental problem becomes more apparent.

WHAT, THEN, IS SCRIPTURE?

Until now this book has proceeded mostly on the basis of subtraction: the identification and removal of what Moshe could not possibly have conceived or imagined, much less thought seriously about. As we have noted, this approach is much easier and more straightforward than trying, at this late date, to determine what Moshe actually thought. This subtraction approach has been fruitful. Perhaps it can be profitably applied to the Hebrew canon as a whole and not just to Moshe's Genesis.

Given what has become evident in the divergence of Ian Michael's narrative path from Moshe's, the first nonviable

5. These are usually termed "temporary hours" to distinguish them from the later sixty-minute hours with which Ian Michael is familiar.

conception of Scripture is *verbal inspiration*, which can be subtracted from the list of options immediately. *Verbal inspiration* is the idea that God's Word is made up of words provided by God to the individual Bible writers. Inerrancy falls into the same category, for even if the Genesis narrators produced an inerrant message, the many intermediate steps between that original message and the one that Ian Michael reads would seem to rule out the possibility that what he holds in his hands is an error-free or verbally dictated text. An entire subdiscipline of Biblical studies called textual criticism is devoted to assessing the variations evident in surviving manuscripts. There are, of course, additional problems inherent in the oral transmission that preceded the written documents as well as the necessity of translation that came later in the history of copies of copies of copies through the centuries.

Another set of problems must also be acknowledged, although we in the twenty-first century can do nothing about them. Not only does some of the supposedly "scientific" information recorded in Genesis 1–11 appear to be so incorrect that it cannot be taken seriously, but some of the theological information appears to be inadequate, and possibly just plain wrong. The Flood narrative describes a God who declares, "I will blot out from the earth the human beings I have created—people together with animals and creeping things and birds of the air, for I am sorry that I have made them" (Gen. 6:7). Apart from the ethical issues involved in the deliberate drowning of children, babies, and puppies, it is difficult to align this scenario with the picture of God provided by Gospel narratives of Jesus of Nazareth. Challenges of this sort must be addressed by any adequate understanding of the nature of Scripture.

As Ian Michael continues to read, he may well note that Genesis 1–11 and beyond does not even attempt to provide him with a set of propositions about God's existence, nature, and character—all of which are essential to an adequate understanding of God (at least that is what Ian Michael's pastor or religion professor would tell him). Rather than a systematic exposition, Genesis is a series of narratives that describe actions of God and human beings. There is little if any moralizing,[6] no drawing of broad theological conclusions; it is mostly straightforward storytelling. Yet there must have been more going on, for this collection of narratives about many generations of people and relationships has survived for millennia and is widely and plausibly regarded as foundational for Western civilization.

WHO GOD IS, WHAT GOD DOES, AND WHAT GOD WANTS FOR US

The basic thesis of this book, as of the two that preceded it, is that in the narratives contained in Scripture and contributed by many different authors over a time span measured in centuries, Moshe, his contemporaries, and their descendants were able (motivated and assisted by the Holy Spirit) to discern essential truths about God. In every time and place this information enlarged and enhanced what the Hebrews—Moshe's kith and kin—understood about God's nature, activity, and intention for humanity. For that reason, the ancient Hebrews first committed the narratives to memory, then preserved them in written form, and eventually copied and recopied them for centuries. As time passed and they derived God-knowledge from the narratives, both the questions they formulated

6. A careful reader of Genesis will note that it is not until chapter 34 that the author provides the first moralizing comment on the events he narrates—and then it is almost as an aside. In reporting the rape of Dinah (the daughter of Jacob by Leah), he notes that "such a thing ought not to be done" (v. 7).

and the answers they discerned enlarged and changed. The Hebrews became more monotheistic and more ethical, and they thought more profoundly about theological issues. The information and insights they gained from the preserved and revered documents continued to be meaningful and enlightening to those who told, retold, and reflected on the narratives of people, events, and times gone by.

Today, however, Ian Michael encounters significant difficulties as he reads translated versions of this curated collection of narratives and resulting insights. These difficulties are by no means the result of malice on the part of translators, whose challenges are, as we have noted, inherent in the nature of their enterprise. But we have by no means exhausted the obstacles that lie in Ian Michael's path. Further "strangeness" awaits him also as he pursues his quest for Biblical understanding.

As we explained in chapter 2 and have subsequently mentioned, Moshe and his tribespeople lived in a two-explanacept world, defining and understanding reality with just two categories of explanation. Lacking a concept of "nature" and specifically "natural regularity," they knew only of "human action" and "divine action." Whatever humans did not do or could not possibly do, God did. Only in such a world could God be assigned responsibility for the way a lot (or a die) landed (Prov. 16:33). All situations in which humans could not have been responsible or in which they were not involved were understood as instances of God-in-action. This was the way the ancient Hebrews experienced everything that happened; for them, that was why what happened, happened. In this sense Genesis is all *theology*, and it is in this sense that it should be read. *Theology* in Moshe's world included not only words and thinking that were explicitly "about God" but also words and thinking about events—such as the Great Flood—that could not have been the result of human decision and action. With no third option besides "human action" and "divine action," God was invoked to account for a wide range of phenomena that Ian Michael knows and understands as "natural occurrences." To modern ears, Moshe's *theology* is so broad as to be extremely confusing, and Ian Michael needs to adapt to the situation as best he can. There is no way for him to change Moshe's conceptual understanding or linguistic practice.

FIRST RETRO-TRANSLATING, THEN ABANDONING THE "NATURE" EXPLANATION

"To begin with God created the sky and the land." As he reads, Ian Michael needs to keep constantly in mind that things he, in the twenty-first century, would interpret as natural events Moshe interpreted as God-in-action. To be true to the text, he must understand it as Moshe understood it—as an account of acts of God. This is difficult, but in fairness to Moshe (as well as for his own understanding), Ian Michael needs to do it. After all, the text he is trying so hard to understand in spite of its "otherness" was addressed to and preserved by Moshe. Indeed, Ian Michael has the Hebrew canon *only because* Moshe and his descendants (motivated and guided by the Holy Spirit) found it meaningful and copied it. That they did so through the centuries ensured that these valuable narratives were available when the Hebrew canon was constructed in first-century Palestine.

When Ian Michael reads of a *raqia'* that limits the force and effect of the *tehom*, he must not expostulate, "Nonsense! There is no sky-vault that confines untamed, pre-Creation bodies of water." Rather, he should read Genesis as *theology*—as confirmation that a generous, all-powerful YHWH created the sky and the land as a locus of extraordinary blessing for Moshe and took the necessary preparatory steps to carry this project forward successfully. He should read the Creation narrative as assurance that God maintains the same kind of concern for Ian Michael that God had for Moshe. When Ian Michael reads that a "greater light" was set in the "firmament," he need not picture God physically attaching the sun to the inner surface of some gigantic sky-vault nor understand the statement as a kind of pre-scientific assertion of the sun's location in space. Instead, he can hear God ensuring that Moshe could "tell time," that his crops would grow, and that the produce would feed his children—and find in that reading assurance that God continues to act that way in Ian Michael's twenty-first-century world.

Reading Genesis as *theology* is counterintuitive, especially when it seems to Ian Michael's science-conditioned mind that the Creation narrative is about nature and nature's regularities. But he really has no choice; he is reading a communication that was, like a forwarded email message, addressed to someone else in a completely different context. Still, though not originally *addressed* to Ian Michael, the message of Genesis is most certainly *intended for his benefit*, and it will serve that purpose if he will let it do so. That, however, requires that he read it first as Moshe understood it. Then he can appropriate for himself the God-knowledge the message contains. What he must not do is to read the message as science (or proto-science); it was not science, as Ian Michael understands the term; it was, and will always remain, *theology*.

If, however, Ian Michael recognizes that Genesis 1–11 is *theology*, he will not only succeed in understanding Genesis but will also find it to be extraordinarily rewarding. Encountering a *raqia'* and a *tehom* at the very beginning of Genesis will remind him of the nature and challenge of reading and understanding Genesis. These enigmatic entities will also remind him of the insights and rewards that await his careful reading of the narratives of Genesis 1–11. Like Moshe, he will come to know more clearly who God is, what God does, and what God wants for him—but this time it will be in his own century.

Chapter Eleven

LITERAL, FIGURATIVE—BOTH OR NEITHER?

Ian Michael's Inescapable Conundrum

Ian Michael faces a dilemma every time he opens his Bible. If he is going to read it at all thoughtfully, he will also have to interpret it. He is reading a Bible translated into English since he does not read Hebrew, and he will have to determine what meanings the *translated* text holds for him. He knows that some readers take it as self-evident that God's Word is an English translation of Hebrew words that were actually spoken by God. Being college-educated, however, he knows that serious problems await him if he goes down this path—if he takes the words he reads at "face value" and interprets everything literally.

A "face-value" English reading of the early chapters of Genesis says that planet Earth is young and that plants, animals (including dinosaurs), birds, and human beings came into existence within days of each other. But his college education has almost certainly informed him of evidence (in God's "book of nature," no less) that the Earth is ancient and that its life forms came into existence over long periods of time. He has been told that new life forms appeared periodically as older ones died out, and he has been shown fossils as convincing evidence that some of Earth's creatures became extinct as the millennia passed. Furthermore, his teachers have almost certainly provided scientifically credible evidence to back up their assertions that the Earth is indeed very old. If he believes what he has learned in college, it is clear to him that a literal, face-value reading of his Bible (whatever version he prefers) is problematic.

Ian Michael knows of only one alternative to reading the Bible literally, and he finds it unattractive. That alternative is to read the Bible *figuratively*. Although this approach sidesteps the conflict between apparently verifiable scientific facts and the Genesis narrative of Creation, it presents other problems. Having explored this option during his formative years, Ian Michael is aware that reading the Bible figuratively opens up the question of when (if ever) a face-value reading is appropriate and when he is to understand that what the Bible is saying is metaphor, simile, symbol, or analogy. "Surely," he says to himself, "the descriptions of God's love and goodness are to be taken literally. But if these descriptions of God's character and values are to be taken at face value, why are the descriptions of the Creator's acts to be understood figuratively? Why here but not there?

Perhaps only moral claims are to be read and understood literally. But Ian Michael already knows that this too is problematic. Is God's promise to blot out the Amorites, the

Hittites, the Perizzites, the Canaanites, the Hivites, and the Jebusites and give their territory—the Promised Land—to the Hebrews (Exod. 23:23) not to be taken literally? And, if it *is* to be taken literally and not figuratively, what does that say—dare Ian Michael even ask the question?—about God's morality?

Perhaps Ian Michael should note carefully the kind of literature that is in front of him. After all, God's Word is sometimes unmistakably in the form of poetry, sometimes in song, sometimes in direct prophetic utterance, but most often it is in a story—in narrative accounts of how the ancestors of the Israelite nation met God and were changed by that meeting. Even so, should Ian Michael always interpret poetry figuratively and narrative literally? If not, when is it appropriate for him to move from one mode of interpretation to the other? What is he to make of God's Word when it claims to be reporting the actual words spoken by God, who said, "I will blot out from the earth the human beings that I have created—people together with animals and creeping things and birds of the air, for I am sorry that I have made them" (Gen. 6:7)? If Ian Michael is to switch from one mode of interpretation to the other in order to read and interpret God's Word accurately, how is he supposed to know when and where the switch from one method of interpretation to the other, from figurative to face-value, is to be made?

Moshe, of course, had no such problem. When he listened to God's Word, the questions that so plague Ian Michael did not trouble Moshe in the slightest. Lacking any concept of "nature" and knowing nothing of science (the codification and explication of the "laws of nature"), he could only understand what he heard as God-in-action. The Genesis narratives of Creation were accounts of what God had done to bring Moshe's world—Moshe's reality—into existence. They answered Moshe's questions, "Why am I here?" and "What does this story mean for me and my fellow human beings?" As Moshe listened, he understood the words he heard as a straightforward assertion that God had acted to bring him and his world into being. It was an account of the origin of Moshe's reality. To Ian Michael's ears, Moshe's reality is a strange reality indeed—assuming, of course, that Ian Michael is taking note of the words he is reading in his Bible and asking himself what they could possibly mean.

Moshe's reality was centered around—actually, anchored in—the *'erets*, "the land," over-arched by the *shemayim*, "the sky." Above the sky and below the land was still the *tehom*, the primeval pre-Creation water, sometimes called "the Deep." It was there before God began the work of Creation, and for that reason, on the second day of creation, God set in place a *raqia'* to ensure that the *tehom* stayed where, for Moshe's sake, it needed to be confined. For all future time, the *tehom* was to remain, safely, far above the sky and below the land. Furthermore, the "greater light" that God had created was set in the *raqia'* to illuminate and thus serve Moshe's land. The "greater light" traveled from east to west across that land each day and returned to its eastern starting point by traveling under the land each night. That it did so, consistently and reliably, was God's doing—divinity acting for Moshe's benefit. All this was not *science*; it was *theology*.

As he listened, did Moshe interpret the words of the narrative literally? Of course. However, if he had been asked the question directly, "Do you take the Genesis account at face value?" he probably would have responded, "What in the world do you mean by that?"

So, if Moshe interpreted the words of Genesis literally—and it was to Moshe that Genesis was addressed—perhaps

Ian Michael's interpretive dilemma is largely due to his failure to recall the nature of the Bible he is reading. If Moshe had no problem hearing the words of Genesis and interpreting them—literally, when they were so intended, poetically when that was their genre, and ethically when a prophet spoke—why isn't Ian Michael able to do the same? Why can't he interpret the Bible literally when the author appears to have intended his words be taken at face value?

The answer, of course, lies in the differences that the passing of three thousand years has made in the world in which Ian Michael finds himself as he reads the very same words. After all, these were the words that, taken at face value by Moshe, so effectively answered his *existential* questions. However, Ian Michael will be profoundly disappointed if he expects that Genesis read literally is going to answer his scientific questions about the origins of the planet on which he lives and the sun around which it circles.

In Ian Michael's twenty-first-century Western world, the sun is not subservient to Earth; planet Earth is entirely dependent on the sun. There is no pre-Creation *tehom* above Ian Michael's sky and no *raqia'* to keep it there and prevent it from flooding Ian Michael's Earth. Science has eliminated the possible existence of a *tehom* or a *raqia'*. Having been convinced that Earth hangs in empty space, held there by gravity, Ian Michael knows, in spite of what his eyes tell him, that the sun doesn't actually go overhead each day and underneath each night. He is very much aware that Earth is constantly moving, rotating on its axis once every twenty-four hours, its surface turning at more than a thousand miles an hour—and at the same time orbiting the immensely larger sun at more than a thousand miles a *minute*.

Ian Michael's Bible-reading dilemma, poised as he is between a literal or a figurative interpretation, is a problem only because he fails to pursue diligently enough an alternative, quite reasonable, and rational approach. That approach would be to first determine the genre of the text before him and then read it accordingly. When considering how long the earth has existed and wondering whether mammals and dinosaurs appeared on earth simultaneously, Ian Michael is asking questions that are irrelevant to the genre of the text he is reading. So it is not at all surprising that the information he extracts from the text is so puzzling. It will continue to remain puzzling unless and until he changes his approach to reading the Bible (and to reading Genesis in particular).

Addressed to Moshe, Genesis was *theology*, words about God—about who God was, what God did, and what God wanted for humans made in God's image. When it came to talking about the *ultimate origin*—and therefore the *meaning*—of existence in general and human existence in particular, there was no relevant category other than *theology*. There was, of course, the category of human beings and their actions (what Ian Michael calls *anthropology*), but that was clearly irrelevant to questions about the *origin* of humans and *everything else*.

If Genesis was *intended to be theology*, it would be meaningful only to the extent that it is *read as theology* now. Awkward though Ian Michael will inevitably be in his initial attempts, if he respects the text for what it actually is, he will approach it first of all as Moshe did—asking the questions Moshe asked and hearing the answers Moshe heard. Doing these two things puts Ian Michael in an excellent position to determine which of his own persistent questions the Genesis text (and indeed the whole Hebrew Bible) is prepared to answer.

And here is some very good news for Ian Michael—as well as those of us who, as twenty-first-century Christians, read the Bible seriously and profit from our reading. Addressed to Moshe, Genesis described the divine bringing-into-being of Moshe's *geocentric* world of *'erets* ("land") and *shemayim* ("sky"), protected from the pre-Creation *tehom* ("a primeval abyss of water") by a *raqia'* ("dome"). That is, it explained why there was "something rather than nothing" not scientifically but theologically; from start to finish it was an account of divine action. As such, it cannot conflict with what Ian Michael has learned in college; for everything he encountered there was about natural regularities—a category that came into human consciousness millennia after Moshe walked the dusty paths of his beloved *'erets* (land).

And Moshe's "land" is part of the reason—indeed, it is the main reason—why Ian Michael faces the dilemma of whether the Bible should be read literally or figuratively. Overlooking (or perhaps forgetting) the fact that Moshe's world was very different from theirs, and certainly trying to be as helpful as possible to Ian Michael, modern translators have rendered the Hebrew text so that it sounds as if Genesis is describing the creation of Ian Michael's world. To this end they have translated *raqia'* as "expanse," knowing that Ian Michael will probably read it as "atmosphere" or simply "space." They have consistently rendered *'erets* as "earth," knowing that Ian Michael will almost certainly read it as "Earth," his home planet. By translating *shemayim* as "heavens" and not retaining the clear Hebrew insistence that the "greater light" was "set" in the "dome" that rotated around the "land," they have virtually guaranteed that Ian Michael will misread Genesis. They have made it quite likely that he will read it as a proto-scientific account of the origin of his modern heliocentric world rather than a theological explanation of the reason for an ancient geocentric one.

Returning to our original question—is a literal, face-value reading of Genesis or a figurative reading the only possible way a modern, college-educated Bible reader like Ian Michael can take the Genesis Creation narratives seriously? The answer, we suggest, is for him to keep in mind that he is reading a divine-human communication initially addressed to Moshe and preserved by him so that Ian Michael could consult (and be edified by) it millennia later. He should further keep in mind that this curated collection of sacred writings was not preserved by chance; it was preserved because it answered Moshe's existential questions.

Although the preserved text was not initially addressed to Ian Michael, it is very much worthwhile for him to read it. But as he reads, he must remember that he is reading a forwarded message that was not originally addressed to him. If he does this, he can profit greatly from reading it thoughtfully in the twenty-first century. However, his first step in determining what the Biblical text means is to determine what it meant to Moshe; only then can he adequately understand its message for himself now. He can certainly read the narratives of Creation and of the Great Flood "literally"; and he certainly should do so. However, before taking the text he is reading "at face value," he must put himself mentally, emotionally, and conceptually in Moshe's place because it was to Moshe that Genesis was first addressed. That is a challenging task, but one that Ian Michael will find richly rewarding.

Chapter Twelve

THE FIRMAMENT (*RAQIA'*) AND THE DEEP (*TEHOM*)

In this final chapter, we return to two Hebrew words that vividly illustrate the Bible translator's dilemma. Because of translators' choices, these two words have changed the significance of the best-known Genesis narratives; for these words are pivotal in determining how the narratives of both the Creation and the Great Flood are now understood. Furthermore, it is in the light of these epochal Hebrew stories that Ian Michael can most authentically enter the world of the ancient Hebrews and from that vantage point read and interpret the text that makes up the Hebrew Bible. These two words can help explain why Ian Michael experiences so much difficulty as he attempts to enter Moshe's strange world.

We have already noted (in chapter 7) two words that feature prominently in the Creation narrative and that present themselves to Ian Michael almost before he has begun his journey of Biblical discovery. But ironically, these two words are almost never *seen* by those who read Genesis in the twenty-first century. This oversight is unfortunate because these words represent two realities that played major roles in Moshe's thinking and are crucial clues to his understanding of God's action in Creation and beyond. (Indeed, Genesis 1–11 is mainly about God's motivations and actions in Creation and the Great Flood.)

When we modern Bible readers use Moshe's understanding as our guide to the meaning of Genesis 1–11, we are struck by the profound otherness of his world. But as we look over Ian Michael's shoulder as *he* reads the narratives, we notice that the Genesis world through which he mentally travels is not very strange at all. (He is, of course, reading a recently translated version, not a retro-translation.) Ian Michael does encounter a few surprises, but generally, the world he imagines Moshe inhabiting and the world in which he (Ian Michael) lives do not appear to be all that different. As we have noted, the reason for this state of affairs is related to the diligent efforts of translators to make the Genesis world as understandable, as not strange, as possible to contemporary readers. The less startling the translated text, the more likely a modern reader will feel at home with it, understand it, be blessed by it—and eventually acquire a copy.

HIDING IN PLAIN SIGHT AS "FIRMAMENT" IS THE NONEXISTENT *RAQIA'*

The word *firmament* (*raqia'*) denotes a reality that was prominent in Moshe's conceptual world but doesn't exist at all in Ian Michael's. Furthermore, to the extent that Ian Michael does get a glimmer of meaning from the word, he is pretty sure that the entity it describes never did exist—Moshe notwithstanding. How is this possible? How can the entity called firmament be meaningless to Ian Michael (and to most modern Bible readers) and yet have been so important to Moshe that he was not at all surprised to find that in the process of Creation God gave it "primacy of place" in the order of created entities?

Firmament, as we have already noted, is not really a *translated* word at all—it is a transliterated one. It comes from the Latin *firmamentum*. In the process of transliteration, a new English word (a neologism) is created; but it is a word without meaning because it has no history of usage in English sentences. Whatever meaning the English-spelled foreign-language word subsequently acquires, it acquires by usage.

For this reason, Ian Michael faces formidable obstacles as he tries to make sense out of the word *firmament*. Neither he nor any of his conversation partners are likely to use *firmament* outside of its Biblical setting because none of them believes that such an entity now exists. Ian Michael may well have memorized Psalm 19:1 as a child: "The heavens are telling the glory of God, and the firmament proclaims [KJV: "sheweth"] his handiwork"); but that would probably be the only meaningful sentence that he or his friends could construct containing the word *firmament*. The result is a catch-22 situation: the transliterated word *firmament* has no generally recognized meaning because it is seldom if ever used in ordinary English sentences, and that is because it has no generally recognized meaning. Furthermore, it is unlikely to acquire meaning in the future because those familiar with it from Psalm 19:1 are unlikely to use it outside of its Biblical settings—nor do they usually know what it means even *in* those settings.[1]

In a Latin sentence where *firmamentum* does have meaning acquired from usage, it connotes a strengthening, support, buttress, underpinning—something strong and substantial upon which other things can safely rest. In rhetoric it is sometimes used to designate the main point—the foundation—of an argument. In practice, however, English speakers encounter *firmament* only when they read the Bible. Detached as it is from usage elsewhere, the word is meaningless, and thus the entity it identifies is "hidden in plain sight." That entity (*firmament*) is denoted by a familiar word that doesn't actually *have* any real *meaning* since no one knows what it means; and if Ian Michael doesn't know what he is talking about when he uses the word in connection with Creation, then the entity it connotes in Hebrew—the *raqia'*—is well hidden indeed.[2]

The Latin rendering of *raqia'* as "*firmamentum*" was not the first time translators had attempted to make this enigmatic entity understandable in a language other than Hebrew. Two or more centuries before Christ, when bilingual Jews in Alexandria translated the Hebrew Bible into Greek (creating the Septuagint), they translated *raqia'* as *stereoma*. This word, as used in Greek sentences, not surprisingly carries connotations similar to those of *firmamentum*. Paul uses

---

1. In KJV: Gen. 1:6, 7 (3×), 8, 14, 15, 17, 20; Pss. 19:1; 150:1; Ezek. 1:22, 23, 25, 26; 10:1; Dan. 12:3.

2. As has been anonymously (but correctly) noted, "*Words* don't mean; *people* mean." The meaning of a word comes not so much from its origin (etymology) as from its usage, with the consequence that a word has *no intrinsic meaning*. When the usage of a word changes (as in the recent case of the English word *cool*), its meaning also changes. This is one reason for the importance of new editions of dictionaries as well as new translations of the Bible.

stereoma to describe the firmness, steadfastness, and constancy that should characterize a Christian's faith (Col. 2:5). Here *stereoma* can be safely understood as similar to *firmamentum*—something strong and substantial upon which other things can safely rest. Elsewhere in Greek, *stereoma* was sometimes used to describe the solid front of a disciplined army in battle array.

The continuing obscurity of the Hebrew *raqia'*—in spite of (or perhaps because of) its translation as the Greek *stereoma*, the Latin *firmamentum*, and, beginning with Wycliffe's Bible, the English *firmament*—symbolizes the strangeness that Genesis 1–11 should convey to Ian Michael and his contemporaries but usually fails to do. It fails because of the choices of English translators in a praiseworthy effort to make the Bible approachable and relevant to its modern Western readers.

So what did Moshe understand when he heard of a *raqia'* that was the first actual "thing" that God created and the only reality of any kind created on Creation Day Two? And why did God create a *raqia'* so early in the Creation process? It must have been important, for it was mentioned over and over again as the creation story unfolded.[3]

Etymology may be helpful here. While the meaning of a word is determined by its usage and the usage of *raqia'*, as understood by both Greek and Latin translators, confirms that *raqia'* meant firmness, support, a solid underpinning, *raqia'* does have a cognate Hebrew verb, *raqa'*, which occurs eleven times in Scripture.[4] As we have seen, wherever this verb occurred in Moshe's sacred scrolls, it meant to beat or hammer

3. *Raqia'* occurs nine times in the fifteen verses of Gen 1:6–20.

4. Exod. 39:3; Num. 16:39; 2 Sam. 22:43; Job 37:18; Ps. 136:6; Isa. 40:19; 42:5, 44:24; Jer. 10:9; Ezek. 6:11; 25:6.

or stomp out. The material that was beaten, hammered, or stomped out was usually (though not necessarily) metal. Thus a plausible English translation of *raqia‘* based on its etymology is "a strong and substantial beaten-out (metal) sky-dome" or "a beaten out, strong, and durable sky-vault."

Understandably but unfortunately, ever since Wycliffe's Bible appeared in the fourteenth century, *raqia‘* has almost always been translated as firmament and thus "hidden in plain sight." If *raqia‘* had been more revealingly translated in early English versions with an English word such as *dome* or *vault*, Genesis would be better understood than it now is. Dome and vault already had clear meanings because they were commonly used in English sentences. On the other hand, however, *dome* or *vault* would have seemed quite strange to Ian Michael. From the very first time that he read his Bible as a child, he would have discovered that on Creation Day Two God created a firm, substantial, sky-vault and that it divided the waters above the vault from the waters below it. The Genesis "world" would have seemed a very strange place right from the fifth verse of Genesis 1, and he could not have avoided its strangeness as he regularly does now.

Six centuries of obscurity, however, may now be coming to an end. In the past twenty-five years, a small but increasing number of English versions have translated *raqia‘* as "dome" or "vault," both of which are "firm" and might well be made of metal.[5] In the waning years of the twentieth century, more recent editions of the popular NIV translated *raqia‘* not

5. The fifty-one English translations available on the Bible Gateway website (accessed July 24, 2017) render *raqia‘* thirteen times each as "firmament" and "expanse"; ten times as "dome"; four times as "space"; three times as "something"; twice each as "vault" and "horizon"; and once each as "canopy," "sky," and "vapors"; and once it is transliterated as "raki'a."

with "firmament" or "expanse" but rather with the clearly understandable word "vault."

Translating *raqia'* as "dome" or "vault" emphasizes the "otherness" of Genesis as Ian Michael reads it. That is because Ian Michael and all of his contemporaries know that there is not now nor was there ever such a thing as a sky-dome or sky-vault, and it seems unthinkable that God's Word would assert its existence, even anciently. By rendering *raqia'* as "firmament," translators have technically performed their appointed task—translation—but in the process have "domesticated" Genesis because the actual meaning of *raqia'* has been effectively hidden in plain sight for close to six hundred years.

THE AWESOME TEHOM BECOMES SIMPLY "THE DEEP"

Firmament is not the only translated word by which the "strangeness" of Genesis has been obscured; "the deep" is the traditional English rendering of the Hebrew *tehom* in Genesis 1:2 and elsewhere.[6] This word referred to a reality that caused Moshe serious concern. Genesis indicates not only that it existed before Creation but that it in some sense stood athwart the Creator's path forward. As Moshe understood the Creation story, God needed to contain the *tehom* before creating Moshe's sky and land. Moreover, Moshe knew that it was not eliminated when God "contained" it during Creation but had just been confined by the *raqia'*. Since the *tehom* still

6. The fifty-one translations mentioned in the preceding note render *tehom* twenty-eight times as "deep"; five times as "ocean"; twice each as "deep water," "deep waters," "waters," and "watery depths"; and once each as "abyss," "deep sea," "depth," "ocean depths," "roaring ocean," "very great deep," "watery deep," and "waves"; and twice leave it essentially untranslated.

existed, it might break out again; in fact, it had already done so once before, at the time of the Great Flood.

Such was the "strangeness" of Moshe's world that has to be dealt with if Ian Michael is to find meaning and comfort as he reads Genesis. He knows that there is no water-reality confined to its proper place by a sky-vault above his head. Yet that is what Genesis seems to be saying because that is what Moshe heard in the Genesis narrative. It would be indeed strange if Ian Michael's English version of Genesis read that way, so it doesn't. *Tehom* is usually translated as "the deep," which is a vague entity that is not frightening at all. "The deep" comes across as an awesome but reliable (and thus somewhat reassuring) entity that would hardly be capable of producing a Flood—a Flood, moreover, that destroyed almost all living humans along with all but a very few air-breathing animals.

Thus the translations read by a curious and inquisitive Ian Michael, while they have rendered every Hebrew word into English, have largely obscured much of the strangeness of Moshe's world. With the best of intentions, the translators have "saved" Genesis for modern readers by obscuring the startling world that is actually described in the Hebrew text.

IN "SAVING" GENESIS WE HAVE MISTREATED IT BADLY

Hebrew scholars everywhere consult the fifteen-volume *Theological Dictionary of the Old Testament* (TDOT)[7] whenever they are confronted with what a particular Hebrew word or phrase might mean. It is the "go-to" reference work for all such questions. Under the entry for *'erets* an inquiring

7. G. Johannes Botterweck, Helmer Ringgren, and Heinz-Josef Fabry, eds., *Theological Dictionary of the Old Testament*, trans. John T. Willis, Geoffrey W. Bromley, David E. Green, and Douglas W. Stott, 15 vols. (Grand Rapids: Eerdmans, 1974–2006).

scholar will find the following explanation that (inadvertently) clarifies in a brief two-word phrase why Genesis 1–11 has been so pervasively misunderstood in the modern world: In the Old Testament "*'erets* combines the same nuances of meaning as the related words discussed above: *'earth' in the cosmic sense* as an antithesis to 'heaven,' 'land' in antithesis to 'sea.'"[8] With this statement the TDOT author implies that a "cosmic sense" for *'erets* is very much a possibility in the Old Testament text, and, of course, the premier location for such a "sense" to appear is in Genesis 1–11. The TDOT clearly approves of the practice followed by all English translations beginning with Wycliffe's Bible, for all have translated *'erets* as "earth" in Genesis 1:1, and wherever possible they have done so in the rest of Genesis 1–11.[9]

But it is the translation of *'erets* as "earth" instead of "land" and the rendering of *shemayim* as "heavens" instead of "sky" in Genesis 1:1 that gives the Creation story its "cosmic sense." Every Bible reader, Bible translator, and TDOT contributor knows what is meant by "cosmic sense." That, however, could not have been true for Moshe. He could not have comprehended the meaning of the phrase *cosmic sense* and could not have had anything approaching a "cosmic sense." It was not possible for anyone in Moshe's time (or for centuries thereafter) to have a "cosmic sense."

Moshe knew of his sky and land and of the "lights in the dome of the sky" (Gen. 1:14), including the "greater

8. Magnus Ottosson, *'erets*, in *Theological Dictionary of the Old Testament*, 1:393; emphasis added.

9. Of the eighty-five occurrences of *'erets* in Gen. 1–11, all but eleven are translated "earth." The exceptions are instances where it cannot be translated as "earth" and still have the sentence make sense, as in Gen. 10:20: "These are the sons of Ham, after their tongues, in their ['earths'], and in their nations" (KJV).

light" that warmed and lighted the land and made it fertile, and he knew of the "lesser light" and the stars, but there was nothing approaching a "cosmic sense" in that understanding of reality. Almost all of us (Ian Michael's scientific and theological contemporaries) are the ones who, having a well-developed "cosmic sense" thanks to powerful telescopes and space explorations, have simply assumed that Moshe had a similar view of how the earth and the sun, along with other planetary spheres, were arranged in deep space. We moderns are the ones who have taken it for granted that Genesis 1–11 is in the Bible to answer our cosmological questions and are disappointed when it fails to give us up-to-date, scientifically credible, "cosmological" answers.

Genesis has not done that for us; that was not its purpose. Rather, Genesis was composed to answer Moshe's questions, and Moshe's questions were not in any sense about astronomical science. As we noted in the foreword to this volume, Moshe's questions were exclusively theological, concerned entirely with the *why* of Creation and not at all with the *how*. If queried about the content of his "cosmology," his response would have been the Hebrew equivalent of "Huh?"

In short, Genesis is not at all defective because it fails to provide cosmological answers. It was never intended to do so.

THE GOOD NEWS IN GENESIS

The good news is that centuries-old religion-science controversies—which have been variously labeled as anything from tensions and sibling rivalries to battles and wars[10]—turn out to have been unnecessary; the unfortunate (and culturally and religiously expensive) results of inadequate understandings

10. See, for example, Andrew Dickson White, *A History of the Warfare of Science with Theology in Christendom* (New York: Appleton, 1896).

of both Scripture and truth. For Scripture is God's *Word* but not God's *words*—a transcendently divine message conveyed in inescapably human (and therefore imperfect), culturally conditioned language—in Moshe's language and expressing Moshe's cultural concerns. For example, the Ten Commandments (Exod. 20:3–17) are addressed to men and not to women. For one thing, the second-person singular pronoun, translated as "thou" in Elizabethan English and "you" in modern English, is explicitly male in Hebrew (Hebrew can do that, but English cannot). And for another thing, even in English the tenth commandment is unequivocally addressed to males: "You shall not covet your neighbor's wife" (Exod. 20:17b). To communicate effectively with humanity, God must use human language. All human beings necessarily *think in their own language.*

Two factors, however, complicate the situation. One is the impressiveness of modern science—which has, among other achievements, successfully addressed many physical diseases and thus substantially lengthened human life expectancy, produced spectacular examples of space explanation, and made laptop computers and cell phones into household necessities. Given these accomplishments, especially in his more spiritual moments, Ian Michael finds it very difficult to recognize that there is no science in Genesis—surely that cannot be the case? The other factor is the common and understandable association of science—especially biological science—with atheism, since it seems to disregard God's Word so flagrantly.[11] Given that the Bible is God's Word, it must surely contain remedies, overwhelmingly convincing

11. See, for example, Henry M. Morris, *The Long War Against God: The History and Impact of the Creation/Evolution Conflict* (Grand Rapids: Baker, 1989); Richard Dawkins, *The God Delusion* (Boston: Houghton Mifflin, 2006). Charles Darwin, however, was an agnostic rather than an atheist.

arguments in support of divinely infused science. If that is true (and surely it has to be true), then Genesis must be the "go-to" place to find the antidote to "atheistic science."

But Genesis 1–11 is not a primitive, inadequate "biology" with faults and deficiencies coming from the time and place in which it originated. It was never intended to be cosmology either; it is *we* modern readers (including scholars) who have made it seem so. *We* have done this continually in the past four hundred years as our understandings of biology and cosmology have developed, expanded, and matured. With the best of intentions, *we* have tried to make Genesis *meaningful*, to help it provide scientifically relevant answers to *our* questions. We have sought to do this by translating it in such a way that its purpose now appears to be the provision of biological and cosmological information—of how, and how long ago, animal life came into existence, and when planet Earth, the solar system, and, for that matter, the entire universe originated.

But the function of Genesis 1–11 was—and *is*—far more profound. Three millennia ago its message to Moshe was that all Creation, including Moshe himself, was the result of freely chosen action by a loving God, and that therefore Moshe's existence could have—and did have—ultimate meaning. Because we have so badly misunderstood the message of the Genesis narratives, we have established "Creation" museums, study groups, and research organizations devoted to proving that Genesis is scientifically "accurate" and confirms twenty-first-century understandings. In so doing we have inadvertently substantiated the profoundly mistaken notion that Genesis was written as cosmological and biological science and should be understood accordingly. This is a *modern mistake*; it is not a mistake of Genesis. We have tried to make Genesis do what it cannot do and was never intended to do. Thus we have ensured that the vast majority of twenty-first-century readers will wrongly suppose that the purpose of Genesis 1–11 was and still is to provide *scientific* information.

In attempting to "save" Genesis 1–11, we moderns have mistreated it. It was composed to give Moshe and other ancient Hebrews an interpretation of *human* reality in relation to *ultimate* reality; it was theological anthropology. It was to answer his questions about whether or not his life had *meaning*, and if so, *why*. It was to clarify for him that the underlying purpose of his existence was to actualize God's love. That Genesis 1–11 accomplished its purpose is surely the reason Moshe treasured it so greatly. He and his descendants memorized it, read it to each other, and, by carefully copying it century after century, preserved it for our benefit.

Afterword

THE SURPRISINGLY GOOD NEWS: A REPRISE

In the foreword to this book (as well as the foreword to *God, Sky & Land*) we wrote, "We wish it were otherwise, but there is no getting around the fact that there is a profound disconnect between science (as commonly understood) and Genesis (as usually read), a disconnect that has existed since the scientific revolution began in the sixteenth century."

This disconnect exists because Ian Michael reads Genesis 1–11 in the twenty-first century and assumes that it is describing his own scientific and heliocentric world. When he reads of "the earth" being created in "the beginning," he typically (and understandably) assumes that what is being described is the origin of his home planet, Earth. He thinks he is reading a pre-scientific (or proto-scientific) cosmogony. He takes it for granted that the creation of "the earth" is an integral part of the birth process of a heliocentric system that includes the Earth—and perhaps extends to the birth-process of our whole universe.

Ian Michael reads Genesis 1–11 this way because ever since Wycliffe's Bible was translated into Middle English in the late fourteenth century, the Hebrew word *'erets* has been translated consistently as "earth."[1] Almost certainly this has happened because Earth has been the home planet of the translators, and they pictured a planet called Earth whenever they encountered *'erets* in the creation story. To them, Genesis appeared to describe the coming-into-being of their cosmos, their sun, moon, and stars (even their universe) along with their home planet, Earth. And so *'erets* uniformly became "earth" rather than "land" whenever it was grammatically possible.

This understandable but regrettable decision on the part of all Hebrew-to-English Bible translators has had a far-reaching and highly deleterious effect. It has reinforced the heliocentric cosmology with which all twenty-first-century Bible readers have grown up. Thus Genesis now seems to reflect the modern cosmology that Ian Michael, the college-educated Christian, knows to be pretty accurate. It appears to confirm a heliocentric arrangement with the sun as the gravitational center around which Earth revolves. Ian Michael is therefore understandably nonplussed when the first Creation story as a whole (Gen. 1:1–2:4a) is so problematic scientifically. Combined with James Ussher's chronology,[2] a

1. Of the fifty-one English translations listed by Bible Gateway (biblegateway.com), forty-nine render *'erets* as "earth." The exceptions are the Good News Translation (1992) and the International Standard Version (1995), both of which render *'erets* even more misleadingly as "universe."

2. James Ussher, *Annals of the World*, 1658.

Creation account read in this way indicates a very brief history for the Earth and for life upon it. It also indicates that all life forms—dinosaurs, mammals, and man—came into existence within a two-day period (Gen. 1:20–31). This confrontation between modern science and Genesis-made-modern has proven very distressing to Ian Michael and to his scientifically aware contemporaries.

If, however, Ian Michael reads something like, "To begin with, God created the sky and the land," he will be far more likely to recognize that the Creation narrative he now reads is not, nor has never been, and could not possibly be a description of the origin of the universe known to modern science. Initially intended for Moshe, the narrative was about *the purpose and meaning of Moshe's world*, and it was expressed in language that he could understand—for the obvious reason that "revelation" that is not understood is not a *revelation* at all but pious-sounding gobbledygook.

"Sky" and "land" included everything that Moshe knew about and everything his mind could conceive. In his world, the sun really did go westward over the land during the day (as he saw with his own eyes) and back eastward under the land at night (which was the only available explanation). It was a *geocentric* earth-sun arrangement that, given the time, place, and cultural context of the narrative's composition, could not have been otherwise. Understanding that he is being transported back to Moshe's world and seeing it through Moshe's eyes, Ian Michael is not at all surprised at the rest of the Creation narrative, which details the *meaning* of Moshe's world—and, more particularly, the *meaning and purpose* of Moshe himself.

This is what Moshe most needed to hear, and that is what the divinely inspired narrative gave to him and his posterity. And this is why the Creation narrative must be read not as *pre-* (or *proto-*) *scientific history* (which is the way it is often *mis*read) but *theological anthropology*, an interpretation of *human* reality in relation to *ultimate* reality. Once Ian Michael orients himself to Moshe's time, space, and existential situation—with Moshe's sky above and Moshe's land beneath his feet, he can enter Moshe's existential world as well. Moshe had only two explanatory categories (explanacepts), and *natural science* was not one of them. Ian Michael can (and should) realize that what he reads in Genesis is not and never was *pre-* or *proto-*science at all, but *theological anthropology* through and through; it is about how created reality is related to—or, more precisely, how the created reality *was understood by Moshe* to be related to—the Creating God. Our understanding, along with Ian Michael's, is, of course, immensely enriched by the revelation of God incarnate in Jesus of Nazareth. That is a revelation that Moshe did not have.

Why, then, has the science-religion disconnect that started with the rise of science in the sixteenth century continued into the present, so that it proves extraordinarily perplexing now to Ian Michael as he reads his Bible? The answer to this question—and the cause of this long-running controversy—lies in three *contrary-to-fact assumptions in Ian Michael's head*:

- That *'erets* in the Creation narratives referred to planet Earth, rather than simply to Moshe's beloved "land"—this despite the fact that *'erets* almost always means "land" or "ground" or "country" in the rest of the Hebrew Bible. At the time when Moshe first heard of the divine Creation, Earth-as-planet was still 2,500 years in the future. The Creation narrative was addressed to Moshe, and its subject was (and is) far more important than any science (proto or modern).

- That the first Creation narrative describes the coming-into-being of a heliocentric solar system. It does not. It describes the sun traveling across Moshe's sky by day and under his "land" (or through that "land's" nether regions) by night—an incurably geocentric arrangement; half of which (the daylight half) Moshe could plainly see. Instead, Ian Michael erroneously assumes that the Creation narrative describes the origin of his solar system in which a relatively small earth orbits a gigantic sun.
- That the *raqia'* and the *tehom* can be safely ignored because they were insignificant players in the Creation drama—despite the fact that they appear early and prominently in the narrative, occupying all of Creation Day Two. As the story is told, one of these entities, the *tehom*, impeded the Creation process until God, by creating and deploying the *raqia'*, made it possible for Moshe to be blessed by the appearance of "sky" and "land."

These three assumptions are the (usually unexamined) intellectual heritage of every English translator since the appearance of Wycliffe's Bible. They are certainly the unexamined intellectual heritage of every Bible reader in the last four hundred years who has failed to question why the very same text that confirmed Moshe's geocentric cosmology is now read as a divine establishment of a heliocentric one.

Having sojourned briefly in Moshe's world of "sky" and "land" with a protecting *raqia'* overhead and the worrisome *tehom* safely confined to its proper place, we are not at all surprised if Ian Michael, on returning to his twenty-first-century world, breathes a sigh of relief. This is indeed good news. The disturbing tension in his psyche between what he learned at college and what he reads in Genesis has vanished. Understanding now that the Creation story is not in any sense divinely revealed *proto-science*, he is now aware that the Genesis *theological* narrative *cannot* conflict with science—any more than Franz Schubert's "Ave Maria" can conflict with the physics of sound.

Furthermore, the Creation narrative never really *was* in conflict with the Johnny-come-lately intellectual project called *science*. The Creation story answered Moshe's existential questions about his reality and accounted for the existence of his (geocentric) world. It explained why the sun went westward over the land in the daytime and returned eastward under the land at night. It explained that all these blessings of sky and land and sun, as well as his existence, were the result of YHWH acting creatively for Moshe's own benefit. It confirmed that he existed because an infinitely generous and loving God willed him to be, and that his personal mission was to actualize God's love throughout his lifetime in his own time and place.

THE ILLUSION OF "CREATION SCIENCE"

Creation science is an accepted term of reference that implies that there exists a real and legitimate subdiscipline of science derived from the Creation narrative in Genesis. Such a discipline—if it existed—would have to be undergirded by the Genesis narrative because that narrative provides the only available evidence on the matter. The regularly unvoiced and probably unexamined assumption is that Genesis 1–11 contains scientific facts, data, and observations that, if properly organized and brought up to date, could undergird scientific investigation into cosmic origins—and furthermore, that such investigative activities would meet the accepted scientific standards for research in the twenty-first century.

This assumption, however, is dubious for several reasons, mainly because the category "scientific" is a relatively recent concept. It certainly did not exist in Moshe's day nor for several millennia thereafter. As often emphasized in this trilogy, Moshe had only two explanatory concepts (explanacepts) for all events and entities. These two categories—divine action and human action—explained all known reality. If humans (individually or collectively) did not do or could not have done something, produced something, destroyed something, and so on, the only possible explanation was God. There was no third conceptual category by which facts, data, or observations could be understood. With no conceptual category available with which to think about such matters, there were, as a result, no words to identify or describe them.

This is not to say that there were no "observations" of "natural occurrences" in Moshe's world. To be sure, he and his contemporaries observed thunderheads forming, as well as the effects of gale-force winds on their ripening crops (Moshe was likely a farmer). Today, we dignify these observations as "scientific," but this is only because we have such a category. Moshe did not, so he understood these phenomena to be caused by direct divine action—reported in unmistakable terms not only in Genesis but throughout the Hebrew Bible.

In Moshe's world the occurrence of rain, hail, or snow was not simply "weather," neither were such events just "natural occurrences"; instead, they were among the things that God did. When Rachel did not get pregnant, she blamed her husband. "Give me children," she said, "or else I die." He angrily responded, "Am I in God's stead who hath withheld from you the fruit of the womb?" (Gen. 30:1, 2, KJV). No one at that time and place doubted that God was responsible for a woman failing to conceive after sexual intercourse. And God was responsible not only for failure to conceive but also for successful conception. "When the Lord saw that Leah was unloved, he opened her womb" (Gen. 29:31).

In Ian Michael's twenty-first-century world, whether pregnancy occurs after sexual intercourse is a matter of physiology, for which there is a "scientific" explanation. In Moshe's world, however, there were no "scientific explanations" or "natural occurrences," and whether or not a woman became pregnant was a result of God's will and action. The explanation was purely and simply *theological.* If this was the way Moshe thought—as certainly seems to be the case—then the idea of creation *science* is a contradiction in terms. According to the Creation narrative, there were no "natural occurrences"; nothing was the outworking of "natural law"; everything that happened was the result of divine action. No other data are available from Genesis.

Thus "creation science" is a pursuit of a will-o'-the-wisp—an attractive but illusory enterprise.

ANTICIPATING A THEOLOGY OF CREATION

A much more promising project lies immediately at hand—namely, a Biblical theology of Creation. If, as we have insisted throughout this trilogy, the Genesis narratives are not science but theology, serious readers of the Bible, as well as professional scholars, on re-entering Moshe's world, will be able to read the narratives *literally*—as Moshe would have done. In the course of that literal reading, it will become clear that there can be no conflict between a *theological* explanation of the meaning and significance of "first things" and a *scientific* account of when they came to be and what they consist of.

When they are read not as science but as theology, the Genesis narratives will achieve in the twenty-first century the purpose for which they were written originally. That purpose was to convey *theological* understandings: understandings about God; understandings that proved so fraught with meaning that they started the Hebrews on a centuries-long quest to achieve ever clearer insights into God's being, God's actions, and God's intentions. In time, records of that quest came to make up the Hebrew Bible, our Old Testament. Genesis begins that Bible and, more than any other writing, provides the basis for a theology of Creation.

Finite reality is best understood as the gift of a loving God concerned about the flourishing of created reality—especially human reality. Existence itself is a gift for which profound and continuing gratitude in both feeling and action is the only appropriate response. Significantly, feelings of gratitude increase human happiness, and thus human flourishing. Furthermore, divine generosity motivates a human sense of responsibility and generosity in return.

All created reality—material, vegetable, animal, and human—is valuable and deserves proper recognition as the product of divine creativity. Thus a theology of Creation involves respect and concern for every person without regard to gender, race, or status, as well as untiring efforts to protect and promote human health and to develop and improve human intellect. This, in turn, requires the alleviation of homelessness and poverty and ongoing concern for the preservation and improvement of the quality of air and water as vital parts of the Creation given to us by the Creator. All are necessary for human flourishing.

For humans to flourish, this awareness of our creatureliness needs to be constantly reinforced. To that end, the Sabbath is a weekly reminder; indeed, it is the capstone of the Genesis narratives. If humans are to flourish, our existence requires a continuing awareness that we are creatures in the presence of our Creator.

The Creation of human moral agents entailed enormous risk for God, planet Earth, and humanness itself. But God took the risk, saying, "Let us make humanity [Heb., *adam*] in our image, according to our likeness" (Gen. 1:26). Creation was (and still is) a huge divine gamble. The divine gamble in the creation of human moral agents eventually resulted in an enormous cost to God—incarnation, rejection, and death. Perhaps most stunning of all is the realization that the outcome of God's risk, whether God ultimately wins or loses the gamble, is to a large extent up to us human beings.

A logically inevitable implication of *creatio imago Dei* is social inclusiveness:

> So God created humankind in his image,
> in the image of God he created them,
> male and female he created them.
> (Gen. 1:27)

This is a clear affirmation of sexual equality as well as cultural inclusiveness. It is obvious that God believes in both human variety and human oneness.

As for who God is, God is the divine actualization and personification of infinite, unconditional, unending love.

What God does is to express this love in continuing action for the benefit of created reality. What God wants for human reality is its flourishing—the fulfillment of its great potential for love, happiness, and satisfaction.

This, in part, is what a theology of Creation could look like.

BIBLIOGRAPHY

Achtemeier, Paul J., et al. *Harper's Bible Dictionary*. San Francisco: Harper and Row, 1985.

Allen, Don Cameron. *The Legend of Noah: Renaissance Rationalism in Art, Science, and Letters*. Urbana, IL: University of Illinois Press, 1963.

Alter, Robert. *Genesis: Translation and Commentary*. New York: Norton, 1996.

Aronofsky, Darren, and Ari Handel, dirs. *Noah*. 2014. Los Angeles: Paramount Pictures, 2014.

Augustine of Hippo. *The Literal Meaning of Genesis*. Ancient Christian Writers, 41, 42. Translated by John Hammond Taylor. Mahwah, NJ: Newman, 1982.

Bailey, Lloyd R. *Noah: The Person and the Story in History and Tradition*. Columbia, SC: University of South Carolina Press, 1989.

Baldwin, John Templeton, ed. *Creation, Catastrophe, and Calvary: Why a Global Flood Is Vital to the Doctrine of Atonement*. Hagerstown, MD: Review and Herald, 2000.

Bandstra, Barry L. *Genesis 1–11: A Handbook on the Hebrew Text*. Waco, TX: Baylor University Press, 2008.

Bassett, Frederick W. "Noah's Nakedness and the Curse of Canaan a Case of Incest?" *Vetus Testamentum* 21, no. 2 (1971), 232–37.

Bauckham, Richard. *The Bible and Ecology: Rediscovering the Community of Creation*. Sarum Theological Lectures. Waco, TX: Baylor, 2010.

Beaude, Pierre-Marie. *The Book of Creation*. Translated by Andrew Clements. Illustrated by Georges Lemoine. Saxonville, MA: Picture Book Studio, 1991.

Bell, Rob. *What Is the Bible? How an Ancient Library of Poems, Letters, and Stories Can Transform the Way You Think and Feel About Everything*. New York: HarperOne, 1917.

Bergman, Jan, and Magnus Ottosson. "*'erets*." In *Theological Dictionary of the Old Testament*, edited by G. Johannes Botterweck and Helmer Ringgren, translated by John T. Willis, 1:???. Grand Rapids, MI: Eerdmans, 1974.

Berry, R. J. "I Believe in God, Maker of Heaven and Earth." In *Real Scientists, Real Faith*, edited by R. J. Berry, 5–12. Grand Rapids: Monarch, 2009.

Billis, A. G., S. Kastanakis, H. Giamarellou, and G. K. Daikos. "Acute Renal Failure After a Meal of Quail." *The Lancet* 289, no. 7726 (September 25, 1971), 702.

Blocher, Henri. *In the Beginning: The Opening Chapters of Genesis*. Translated by David G. Preston. Downers Grove, IL: InterVarsity, 1984.

Boardman, Donald C. "Did Noah's Flood Cover the Entire World? No." In *The Genesis Debate: Persistent Questions about Creation and the Flood*, edited by Ronald F. Youngblood, 210–29. Grand Rapids: Baker, 1990.

Boice, James Montgomery. *Genesis: An Expositional Commentary*. 3 vols. Grand Rapids, MI: Zondervan, 1982.

Botterweck, G. Johannes, Hilmer Ringgren, and Heinz-Josef Fabry, eds. *Theological Dictionary of the Old Testament*. Translated by John T. Willis, Geoffrey W. Bromley, David E. Green, and Douglas W. Stott. 15 vols. Grand Rapids: Eerdmans, 1974–2006.

Boyd, Gregory A. *God of the Possible: A Biblical Introduction to the Open View of God*. Grand Rapids, MI: Baker, 2000.

Brown, William P. *The Ethos of the Cosmos: The Genesis of Moral Imagination in the Bible*. Grand Rapids, Eerdmans, 1999. See especially, "Noah: Moral Man in Immoral Society," 174–81.

Brueggemann, Walter. *Genesis*. Interpretation: A Bible Commentary for Teaching and Preaching. Louisville, KY: John Knox, 1982.

Bull, Brian S., and Fritz Guy. *God, Land, and the Great Flood: Hearing the Story with 21st-Century Christian Ears*. Roseville, CA: Adventist Forum, 2017.

————. God, Sky and Land: Genesis 1 as the Ancient Hebrews Heard It. Roseville, CA: Adventist Forum, 2011.

Burke, James. *The Day the Universe Changed*. Boston: Little, Brown, 1985.

Cassuto, Umberto. *A Commentary on the Book of Genesis, Part One: From Adam to Noah*. Translated by Israel Abrahams. Jerusalem: Magnes/Hebrew University, 1978.

Chen, Y. S. *The Primeval Flood Catastrophe*. Oxford Oriental Monographs. New York: Oxford, 2013.

Christensen, Duane. "The Lost Books of the Bible." *Bible Review* 14, no. 5 (October 1998).

Cohn, Norman. *Noah's Flood: The Genesis Story in Western Thought.* New Haven, CT: Yale University Press, 1996.

Collins, C. John. *Genesis 1–4: A Linguistic, Literary, and Theological Commentary*. Phillipsburg, NJ: Presbyterian and Reformed, 2006.

Cornell, T. J. *The Beginnings of Rome: Italy and Rome from the Bronze Age to the Punic Wars* (c. 1000–264 bc). New York: Routledge, 1995.

Cotter, David W. *Genesis.* Berit Olam Studies in Hebrew Narrative & Poetry. Collegeville, MN: Liturgical Press, 2003.

Cottrell, Raymond C. "Extent of the Genesis Flood." In *Creation Reconsidered: Scientific, Biblical, and Theological Perspectives,* edited by James L. Hayward, 265–77. Roseville, CA: Adventist Forum, 2000.

Crossan, John Dominic. *How to Read the Bible and Still Be a Christian.* New York: HarperOne, 2015.

Custance, Arthur C. *The Flood: Local or Global?* His The Doorway papers, Vol. 9. Grand Rapids: Zondervan, 1979.

Davidson, Richard M. "Biblical Evidence for the Universality of the Genesis Flood." In *Creation, Catastrophe, and Calvary: Why a Global Flood Is Vital to the Doctrine of Atonement,* edited by John Templeton Baldwin. 79–93. Hagerstown, MD: Review and Herald, 2000.

Doukhan, Jacques. "The Literary Structure of the Genesis Creation Story." ThD diss., Andrews University, 1978.

Dundes, Alan, ed. *The Flood Myth.* Berkeley, CA: University of California Press, 1988.

Eichrodt, Walter. "In the Beginning: A Contribution to the Interpretation of the First Word of the Bible." In *Creation in the Old Testament,* edited by Bernhard W. Anderson, 65–73. Philadelphia: Fortress, 1984.

Falk, Marcia. "Translation as a Journey." In *The Song of Songs: A New Translation and Interpretation,* 91–98. San Franscisco: Harper, 1990.

Finkel, Irving. *The Ark Before Noah: Decoding the Story of the Flood.* New York: Doubleday, 2014.

Fox, Everett. *The Five Books of Moses: Genesis, Exodus, Leviticus, Numbers, Deuteronomy: A New Translation with Introductions, Commentary, and Notes*. New York: Schocken, 1997.

Fretheim, Terence E. *Creation, Fall, and Flood: Studies in Genesis 1–11*. Minneapolis: Augsburg, 1969.

———. "Genesis 1:1–2:3, The Creation." In *The New Interpreter's Bible: A Commentary in Twelve Volumes*, 1:338–47. Nashville: Abingdon, 1994.

———. "Genesis 6:5–8:22—The Flood: The Great Divide." In *God and the World in the Old Testament: A Relational Theology of Creation*, 79–83. Nashville: Abingdon, 2005.

———. "The God of the Flood Story and Natural Disasters." In *Creation Untamed: The Bible, God, and Natural Disasters*, 39–64. Theological Explorations for the Church Catholic. Grand Rapids, MI: Baker, 2010.

———. *The Suffering of God: An Old Testament Perspective*. Overtures to Biblical Theology 14. Philadelphia: Fortress, 1984.

Frymer-Kensky, Tikva. "The Atrahasis Epic and Its Significance for Our Understanding of Genesis 1–9." *Biblical Archaeologist* 40, no. 4 (December 1977), 147–55.

———. "The Flood." In *Harper's Bible Dictionary*, edited by Paul J. Achtemeier, 312–14. San Francisco: Harper and Row, 1985.

George, A. R. "The Tower of Babel: Archaeology, History, and Cuneiform Texts." *Archiv für Orientforschung* 51 (2005/2006), 75–95.

Geraty, Lawrence T. "Archaeology of the Flood Story." In *Understanding Genesis: Contemporary Adventist Perspectives*, edited by Brian Bull, Fritz Guy, and Ervin Taylor, 167–95. Riverside, CA: Adventist Today, 2006.

Gibson, John C. L. *Genesis: Volume 1*. The Daily Study Bible Series. Louisville, KY: Westminster John Knox, 1981.

Gibson, L. James, and Humberto M. Rasi, eds. *Understanding Creation: Answers to Questions on Faith and Science*. Nampa, ID: Pacific Press, 2011.

Gilkey, Langdon B. "What the Idea of Creation Means." In *Maker of Heaven and Earth: The Christian Doctrine of Creation in the Light of Modern Knowledge*, 41–80. Garden City, NJ: Doubleday, 1965.

Glover, Gordon J. *Beyond the Firmament: Understanding Science and the Theology of Creation*. Chesapeake, VA: Watertree, 2007.

Gorg, M. "*raqia'*." In *Theological Dictionary of the Old Testament*, edited by G. Johannes Botterweck, Helmer Ringgren, and Heinz-Josef Fabry, translated by David F. Green, 13:646–53. Grand Rapids, MI: Eerdmans, 2004.

Grady, J. Lee. "Seven of the Worst Mistakes in the Movie 'Noah.' " *Charisma News*, April 10, 2014, https://www.charismanews.com/opinion/43454-seven-of-the-worst-mistakes-in-the-movie-noah.

Greenwood, Kyle. *Scripture and Cosmology: Reading the Bible Between the Ancient World and Modern Science*. Downers Grove, IL: IVP Academic, 2015.

Guy, Fritz. "God's Time: Infinite Temporality and the Ultimate Reality of Becoming." *Spectrum* 29, no. 1 (Winter 2001), 19–28.

Halton, Charles, James K. Hoffmeier, Gordon J. Wenham, and Kenton L. Sparks, *Genesis: History, Fiction, or Neither? Three Views on the Bible's Earliest Chapters*. Counterpoints. Grand Rapids, MI: Zondervan, 2015.

Harland, P. J. *The Value of Human Life: A Study of the Story of the Flood (Genesis 6–9)*. Supplements to *Vetus Testamentum* 64. Leiden, Netherlands: Brill, 1996.

Hegel, G. W. F. *Phenomenology of Spirit*. Translated by A. V. Miller. New York: Oxford, 1977.

Heidel, Alexander. *The Babylonian Genesis: The Story of Creation*. 2nd ed. Chicago: University of Chicago Press, 1951.

Hodge, B. C. *Revisiting the Days of Genesis: A Study of the Use of Time in Genesis 1-11 in Light of Its Ancient Near Eastern and Literary Context*. Eugene, OR: Wipf & Stock, 2011.

Horn, Siegfried H. "Firmament." In *Seventh–day Adventist Bible Dictionary*. Commentary Reference Series 8. Washington, DC: Review and Herald, 1960.

Hover–Johag, I. "*tob*." In *Theological Dictionary of the Old Testament*, edited by G. Johannes Botterweck and Helmer Ringgren, translated by David E. Green, 5:296–317. Grand Rapids, MI: Eerdmans, 1986.

Jacob, Benno. *Genesis: The First Book of the Bible*. Edited and translated by Ernest I. Jacob and Walter Jacob. New York: Ktav, 1974.

Jaki, Stanley L. *Genesis 1: Through the Ages*. London: Thomas More, 1992.

Johns, Warren H. "Theology and Geology of the Flood: Moving Beyond Flood Geology." In *Understanding Genesis: Contemporary Adventist Perspectives*, edited by Brian Bull, Fritz Guy, and Ervin Taylor, 151–66. Riverside, CA: Adventist Today, 2006.

Kass, Leon. *The Beginning of Wisdom: Reading Genesis*. New York: Free Press, 2003.

Kidner, Derek. *Genesis: An Introduction and Commentary*. Tyndale Old Testament Commentaries. Downers Grove, IL: InterVersity, 1967.

Koehler, Ludwig, and Walter Baumgartner, eds. *Lexicon in Veteris Testamenti Libros*. Grand Rapids: Eerdmans, 1958.

Lambert, W. C., and A. R. Millard. *Atra-Ḫasīs: The Babylonian Story of the Flood*. Oxford: Clarendon, 1969.

Lamoureux, Denis O. *Evolutionary Creation: A Christian Approach to Evolution*. Eugene, OR: Wipf & Stock, 2008.

Langford, Jerome J. *Galileo, Science, and the Church*. 3rd ed. Ann Arbor, MI: University of Michigan, 1992.

Leibniz, Gottfried. *Theodicy: Essays on the Goodness of God, the Freedom of Man, and the Origin of Evil*. Edited by Austin Farrer. Translated by E. M. Huggard. La Salle, IL: Open Court, 1985.

Lewis, Jack P. *A Study of the Interpretation of Noah and the Flood in Jewish and Christian Literature*. Leiden, Netherlands: Brill, 1968.

Long, Charles H. *Alpha: The Myths of Creation*. Classics in Religious Studies 4. Chico, CA: Scholars Press, 1963.

Löning, Karl, and Erich Zenger. *To Begin With, God Created . . . : Biblical Theologies of Creation*. Collegeville, MN: Liturgical Press, 2000.

Louth, Andrew, ed. *Genesis 1–11*. Ancient Christian Commentary on Scripture: Old Testament 1. Downers Grover, IL: InterVarsity, 2001.

Luther, Martin. *Luther's Commentary on Genesis*. 2 vols. Translated by J. Theodore Mueller. Grand Rapids: Zondervan, 1958.

Martinez, Florentino Carcia, and Gerard F. Luttikhuizen, eds. *Interpretations of the Flood*. Themes in Biblical Narrative 1. Leiden, Netherlands: Brill, 1998.

Mathews, Kenneth A. *Genesis 1–11:26*. New American Commentary: An Exegetical and Theological Exposition of Holy Scripture 1a. Nashville: Broadman and Holman, 1996.

Melanchthon, Philip. "Initia Doctrinae Physicae." *Corpus Reformatorum*, 13:216–17.

Milgrom, Jacob. *Leviticus 23–27: A New Translation with Introduction and Commentary*. The Anchor Bible 3B. New York: Doubleday, 2001.

Mitchell, Stephen. *Genesis: A New Translation of the Classic Biblical Stories*. New York: HarperCollins, 1996.

Mitchell, T. "Flood." In *New Bible Dictionary*, 2nd ed., edited by J. D. Douglas et al., 380–83. Downers Grove, IL: InterVarsity, 1994.

Moltmann, Jürgen. *God in Creation: A New Theology of Creation and the Spirit of God*. The Gifford Lectures, 1984–1985. Translated by Margaret Kohl. San Francisco: Harper & Row, 1985.

Montgomery, David R. *The Rocks Don't Lie: A Geologist Investigates Noah's Flood*. New York: Norton, 2012.

Morris, Henry M. *The Genesis Record: A Scientific and Devotional Commentary on the Book of Beginnings*. Grand Rapids, MI: Baker, 1976.

————. *The Long War Against God: The History and Impact of the Creation/Evolution Conflict*. Grand Rapids, MI: Baker, 1989.

Moyers, Bill D. *Genesis: A Living Conversation*. Edited by Betty Sue Flowers. New York: Doubleday, 1996.

Nichol, Francis D., et al., eds. "Evidences of a Worldwide Flood." *Seventh–day Adventist Bible Commentary*, 1:64–97. Washington, DC: Review and Herald, 1953.

Niehr, H. "*'ereb*." In *Theological Dictionary of the Old Testament*, edited by G. Johannes Botterweck, Helmer Ringgren, and Heinz–Josef Fabry, translated by David E. Green, 11:355–41. Grand Rapids, MI: Eerdmans, 2001.

Noorbergen Rene. *The Ark File*. Mountain View, CA: Pacific Press, 1974.

Numbers, Ronald L. *The Creationists: From Scientific Creationism to Intelligent Design*. Expanded ed. Cambridge, MA: Harvard University Press, 2006.

————, ed. *Galileo Goes to Jail: And Other Myths about Science and Religion*. Cambridge, MA: Harvard University Press, 2001.

————. "Science Without God: Natural Law and Christian Beliefs." In *When Science and Christianity Meet*, edited by David C. Lindberg and Ronald L. Numbers, 265–85. Chicago: University of Chicago Press, 2003.

Oord, Thomas J. *The Uncontrolling Love of God: An Open and Relational Account of Providence*. Downers Grove, IL: InterVarsity Academic, 2015.

Patten, Donald W. *The Biblical Flood and the Ice Epoch: A Study in Scientific History*. Seattle: Pacific Meridian, 1966.

Pinnock, Clark H. *Most Moved Mover: A Theology of God's Openness*. Grand Rapids, MI: Baker Academic, 2001.

Pinnock, Clark, Richard Rice, John Sanders, William Hasker, and David Basinger, *The Openness of God: A Biblical Challenge to the Traditional Understanding of God*. Downers Grove, IL: InterVarsity, 1995.

Pleins, J. David. *When the Great Abyss Opened: Classic and Contemporary Readings of Noah's Flood*. New York: Oxford, 2003.

Polkinghorne, John. *Beyond Science: The Wider Human Context*. New York: Cambridge, 1996.

————. *Faith, Science and Understanding*. New Haven, CT: Yale University Press, 2000.

————. *Scientists as Theologians: A Comparison of the Writings of Ian Barbour, Arthur Peacock, and John Polkinghorne*. London: SPCK, 1996.

Ramm, Bernard. *The Christian View of Science and Scripture*. Grand Rapids, MI: Eerdmans, 1954.

Rehwinkel, Alfred M. *The Flood in the Light of the Bible, Geology, and Archaeology*. St. Louis, MO: Concordia, 1951.

Rice, Richard. *The Openness of God: The Relationship of Divine Foreknowledge and Human Free Will*. Nashville: Review and Herald, 1980. Republished as *God's Foreknowledge & Man's Free Will*. Minneapolis: Bethany House, 1985.

Ross, Allen P. *Creation and Blessing: A Guide to the Study and Exposition of Genesis*. Grand Rapids, MI: Baker, 1988.

Ryan, William, and Walter Pitman. *Noah's Flood: The New Scientific Discoveries About the Event That Changed History*. New York: Simon and Schuster, 2000.

Saebo, M. "*yom*, II–III." In *Theological Dictionary of the Old Testament*, edited by G. Johannes Botterweck and Helmer Ringgren, translated by David E. Green, 6:12–32. Grand Rapids, MI: Eerdmans, 1990.

Sailhamer, John H. *Genesis Unbound: A Provocative New Look at the Creation Account*. Sisters, OR: Multnomah, 1996.

Sanders, John. *The God Who Risks: A Theology of Providence*. Downers Grove, IL: InterVarsity, 1998.

Sarna, Nahum M. *Genesis: The Traditional Hebrew Text with New JPS Translation*. JPS Torah Commentary. Philadelphia: Jewish Publication Society, 1989.

————. *Understanding Genesis: The World of the Bible in the Light of History*. New York: Schocken, 1966.

Speiser, E. A. "The Epic of Gilgamesh." In *Ancient Near Eastern Texts Relating to the Old Testament*, 3rd ed., edited by James B. Pritchard, 72–99. Princeton, NJ: Princeton University Press, 1969.

————. *Genesis*. The Anchor Bible 1. Garden City, NY: Doubleday, 1964.

Stek, John H. "What Says the Scripture?" In *Portraits of Creation: Biblical and Scientific Perspectives on the World's Formation*, edited by Howard J. Van Till et al., 203–65. Grand Rapids, MI: Eerdmans, 1990.

Straus, Leo. "On the Interpretation of Genesis (1957)." In *Jewish Philosophy and the Crisis of Modernity: Essays and Lectures in Modern Jewish Thought*, edited by Kenneth Hart Green, 359–76. Albany, NY: State University of New York, 1997.

Sundbergh, Albert C. " 'The Old Testament of the Early Church' Revisited." In *Festschift in Honor of Charles Speel*, edited by Thomas J. Sienkewicz and James E. Betts. Monmouth, IL: Monmouth College, 1996.

Tarnas, Richard. *The Passion of the Western Mind: Understanding the Ideas That Have Shaped Our World View*. New York: Ballantine, 1991.

Taschen, Benedict. *The Bible in Pictures: Illustrations from the Workshop of Lucas Cranach* (1534). Cologne: Taschen, 2009.

Thomas, D. Winton, ed. *Documents from Old Testament Times*. Translated by Members of the Society for Old Testament Study. New York: Harper and Row, 1961.

Tonstad, Sigve K. *God of Sense and Traditions of Non–Sense*. Eugene, OR: Wipf & Stock, 2016.

Tucker, W. Dennis, Jr. "Firmament." In *Eerdmans Dictonary of the Bible*, edited by David Noel Freedman, Allen C. Myers, and Astrid B. Beck. Grand Rapids: Eerdmans, 2000.

Turner, Laurence A. *Back to the Present: Encountering Genesis in the 21st Century*. Grantham, UK: Autumn House, 2004.

———. *Genesis*. Readings: A New Biblical Commentary. Sheffield, UK: Sheffield Academic, 2000.

Tyndale's Old Testament: Being the Pentateuch of 1530, Joshua to 2 Chronicles of 1537, and Jonah. Translated by William Tyndale. New Haven, CT: Yale University Press, 1992.

Van Andel, Tjeerd H. "Late Quaternary Sea–Level Changes and Archaeology." *Antiquity* 63, no. 241 (December 1989), 733–45.

Von Rad, Gerhard. *Genesis: A Commentary*. Rev. ed. Translated by John H. Marks. The Old Testament Library. Philadelphia: Westminster, 1972.

Von Soden, W., J. Bergman, and M. Saebo, "*yom*." In *Theological Dictionary of the Old Testament*, edited by G. Johannes Botterweck and Helmer Ringgren, translated by David E. Green, 6:???. Grand Rapids, MI: Eerdmans, 1990.

Waltke, Bruce K., with Cathi J. Fredricks. *Genesis: A Commentary*. Grand Rapids, MI: Zondervan, 2001.

Walton, John H., *Ancient Israelite Literature in Its Cultural Context: A Survey of Parallels Between Biblical and Ancient Near Eastern Texts*. Grand Rapids: Zondervan, 1989.

———. *Ancient Near Eastern Thought and the Old Testament: Introducing the Conceptual World of the Hebrew Bible*. Grand Rapids, MI: Baker Academic, 2006.

———. *The Lost World of Genesis One: Ancient Cosmology and the Origins Debate*. Downers Grove, IL: InterVarsity, 2009.

Walton, John H., and D. Brent Sandy. *The Lost World of Scripture: Ancient Literary Culture and Biblical Authority*. Downers Grove, IL: InterVarsity, 2013.

Watts, J. Wash. *A Distinctive Translation of Genesis*. Grand Rapids, MI: Eerdmans, 1963.

Wenham, Gordon J. *Genesis 1–15*. Word Biblical Commentary 1. Waco, TX: Word, 1987.

Westermann, Claus. *Creation*. Translated by John J. Scullion. Philadelphia: Fortress, 1974.

———. *Elements of Old Testament Theology*. Translated by Douglas W. Scott. Atlanta: John Knox, 1982.

———. *Genesis: A Practical Commentary*. Text and Interpretation. Translated by David E. Green. Grand Rapids, MI: Eerdmans, 1987.

Whitcomb, John C. *The World That Perished: An Introduction to Biblical Catastrophism*. Rev. ed. Grand Rapids, MI: Baker, 1988.

Whitcomb, John C., and Henry M. Morris. *The Genesis Flood: The Biblical Record and Its Scientific Implications*. Philadelphia: Presbyterian and Reformed, 1961.

White, Andrew Dickson. *A History of the Warfare of Science with Theology in Christendom* (New York: Appleton, 1896).

White, Ellen G. "Christ Our Hope." *Advent Review and Sabbath Herald*, December 20, 1892, 785.

———. *Education*. Oakland, CA: Pacific Press, 1903.

———. "The Flood." In T*he Story of Patriarchs and Prophets: The Conflict of the Ages Illustrated in the Lives of Holy Men of Old*, 90–104. Washington, DC: Review and Herald, 1958.

———. "The Inspiration of the Prophetic Writers." In *Selected Messages from the Writings of Ellen G. White*, 1:15–23. Washington, DC: Review and Herald, 1958.

———. *The Story of Patriarchs and Prophets: The Conflict of the Ages Illustrated in the Lives of Holy Men of Old*. Oakland, CA: Pacific Press, 1890.

———. *Thoughts from the Mount of Blessing*. Oakland, CA: Pacific Press, 1896.

Whitehead, Alfred North. *Process and Reality: An Essay in Cosmology*. Corrected ed. Gifford Lectures, 1927–1928. Edited by David Ray Griffin and Donald W. Sherburne. New York: Free Press, 1978.

Wilson, Edward O. *Consilience: The Unity of Knowledge*. New York: Knopf, 1998.

———. *Sociobiology: The New Synthesis*. Cambridge, MA: Belknap Press, 1975.

Wilson, Ian. *Before the Flood: The Biblical Flood as a Real Event and How It Changed the Course of Civilization*. New York: St Martin's, 2001.

Wittgenstein, Ludwig. *Philosophical Investigations*. 3rd ed. Translated by G. E. M. Anscombe. New York: Prentice Hall, 1973.

Wright, G. Ernest. *God Who Acts: Biblical Theology as Recital*. Studies in Biblical Theology 8. Naperville, IL: Allenson, 1958.

Wright, J. Edward. "Cosmogony, Cosmology." In *The New Interpreter's Dictionary of the Bible*, edited by Katharine Doob Sakenfeld, 1:?? Nashville: Abingdon, 2006.

Young, Davis A. *The Biblical Flood: A Case Study of the Church's Response to Extrabiblical Evidence*. Grand Rapids, MI: Eerdmans, 1995.

———. *Creation and the Flood: An Alternative to Flood Geology and Theistic Evolution*. Grand Rapids, MI: Baker, 1977.

Young, Edward J. *Studies in Genesis One*. International Library of Philosophy and Theology: Biblical and Theological Studies. Philadelphia: Presbyterian and Reformed, 1999.

INDEX

SCRIPTURE INDEX